7 Second Marketing

Marketing

*How to Use Memory Hooks
to Make You Instantly
Stand Out in a Crowd*

IVAN R. MISNER, PH.D.

7 SECOND MARKETING

How to Use Memory Hooks to Make You Instantly Stand Out in a Crowd

IVAN R. MISNER, PH.D.

Bard Press
Austin, Texas

7 Second Marketing
How to Use Memory Hooks to Make You Instantly Stand Out in a Crowd

Bard Press, Inc.
1515 S. Capital of Texas Highway, Suite 205
Austin, Texas 78746
(512) 329-8373, fax (512) 329-6051

A Paradigm Productions Book.

To order the book, contact your local bookstore or call 1-800-945-3132.

ISBN 1-885167-15-6 trade paperback
ISBN 1-885167-21-0 cloth

Library of Congress Cataloging-in-Publication Data
Misner, Ivan R., 1956-
    Seven-second marketing : how to use memory hooks to make you instantly stand out in a crowd / Ivan R. Misner.
        p.   cm.
    Includes bibliographical references and index.
    ISBN 1-885167-21-0 (hardcover). -- ISBN 1-885167-15-6 (pbk.)
    1. Marketing--Psychological aspects. 2. First impression (Psychology). 3. Word-of-mouth advertising. I. Title.
HF5415. 122.M57   1996
658.8--dc20   96-9716
                                                                          CIP

The author may be contacted at the following address:

Ivan R. Misner, Ph.D.
Business Network Int'l.
199 S. Monte Vista
San Dimas, CA 91773
(800) 688-9394

CREDITS

Developmental Editing: *Jeff Morris*

Copyediting: *Kathy Bork*

Proofreading: *Deborah Costenbader, Laurie Drummond, Sherry Sprague*

Text Design/Production: *Jeff Morris*

Jacket Design: *Archetype, Inc.*

DEDICATION

To my parents,

who many years ago

instilled in me the lesson

that diplomacy is the art

of letting someone else

have your way.

▼

CONTENTS

Acknowledgments   **10**
About the Author   **11**

PART I: GETTING THEIR ATTENTION

Using Memory Hooks to Turbocharge Your Referrals

1 INTRODUCTION TO 7 SECOND MARKETING   **15**

About This Book and the Idea behind It

The Hook ▼ The Book

2 THE MORE THINGS CHANGE . . .   **19**

Why We Resist Mass Marketing and Embrace Word of Mouth

That Was Then ▼ and This Is Now ▼ High Wire
with a Net ▼ Information, Please ▼ The Boom
in Business Networking ▼ Getting the Word Out
▼ Making Yourself Memorable

3 THE ART OF THE INTRODUCTION   **27**

How to Meet Prospects Individually and in Groups

First Impressions ▼ Meeting an Individual
▼ Meeting a Group

4 HOW TO MAKE A MEMORY HOOK   **37**

A Mix-and-Match Guide to the Key Ingredients

How Memory Hooks Are Born ▼ What Makes a
Good Memory Hook? ▼ When and How to Use
a Memory Hook

PART II: MEMORY HOOK THEMES

A Potpourri of Ways to Hook Your Prospect

5 DRAW ATTENTION TO YOUR NAME   **47**

Getting Them to Remember Who You Are

6 HIGHLIGHT YOUR COMPANY NAME   **53**

Connecting Who You Are with What You Do

7 COMMUNICATE YOUR PROFESSION   **61**

Reminding Them of What You Can Do for Them

8 TELL THEM QUALITY IS IMPORTANT TO YOU   **85**

Showing Them You're Serious about Your Work

9 EDUCATE AS YOU SELL   **93**

Telling Them What Your Business Does

10 RHYME IT OR SING IT   **101**

Making Them Hum Your Ad for Hours

11 PLAY WITH THE WORDS   **123**

Getting Them to Laugh as They Hand Over Their Business

12 TAKE THE NEXT STEP   **143**

Using What You've Learned

PART III: HANDS ON

Tools to Help You Create and Share Your Own Memory Hook

Notes   **149**

Worksheets   **153**

Index of Memory Hooks by Profession   **155**

About Business Network Int'l.   **159**

▼
ACKNOWLEDGMENTS

F IRST, I WOULD LIKE TO THANK the Southern California Directors and Board of Advisors for BNI, who suggested the idea for this book at our annual Arrowhead meeting last year. Next, I want to acknowledge Andra Brack, Virginia Devine, Norm Dominguez, Chris Means, Shelli Prochaska, Robert Smith, and Bob Sutterfield for their quick and helpful feedback on my manuscript.

Of course, a very big thanks must go to the over two thousand business professionals who mailed, faxed, e-mailed, and handed me their memory hooks during this process. I thoroughly enjoyed reviewing and selecting from this wealth of information and look forward to receiving more.

I would also like to thank all my office staff, headed by Amy Brown, for minding the store while I took time out of the office to complete this book, and my secretary, Roxy Roberson, for compiling many of the memory hooks and their stories for me to work with.

As always, the editing, suggestions, and support that my wife, Elisabeth, provided (not to mention her willingness to let me be "in my cave" while working on this project) are very much appreciated. And for the second time and undoubtedly not the last, I would like to recognize the special efforts of Ray and Scott Bard of Bard Press for their expertise and their commitment to excellence.

Finally, and most importantly, a monumental thank you to Jeff Morris, whose substantial assistance on this project allowed this book to be completed.

Ivan R. Misner, Ph.D.
La Verne, California
June 1996

▼
ABOUT THE AUTHOR

D R. IVAN R. MISNER is the founder and president of Business Network Int'l. in San Dimas, California. Internationally recognized as networking's guru, Dr. Misner is a motivational keynote speaker for major corporations and associations throughout North America. He has been featured in the *Wall Street Journal, Los Angeles Times, New York Times, Entrepreneur* magazine, and numerous television and radio shows across the continent.

Dr. Misner's Ph.D. was earned at the University of Southern California with a specialization in Organizational Development. His doctoral dissertation was on business development networks, and he has published many other books, articles, and tapes on management and networking, including the bestselling book *The World's Best Known Marketing Secret.*

Dr. Misner is on the faculty of business administration at Cal Poly University, Pomona, and is in *Who's Who of Leading American Executives.* He is on the board of directors for the LeRoy Haynes Center, a nonprofit program for abused and neglected children.

In addition, Dr. Misner has been nominated twice for *Inc.* magazine's "Entrepreneur of the Year" award.

Dr. Misner resides in La Verne, California, with his wife, Elisabeth, and three children, Ashley, Cassie, and Trey.

Part

1

Getting
Their Attention

*Using Memory Hooks to
Turbocharge Your Referrals*

PART I

CHAPTER 1
Introduction to 7 Second Marketing

▼

CHAPTER 2
The More Things Change . . .

▼

CHAPTER 3
The Art of the Introduction

▼

CHAPTER 4
How to Make a Memory Hook

Chapter

1

Introduction to 7 Second Marketing

*About This Book
and the Idea behind It*

WHAT SELLS? You've heard many answers to this question, and many of them are true. To sell efficiently and effectively, though, nothing works better than getting others to spread the word on your behalf.

Toward this end, I founded Business Network Int'l. in 1985 as a way for business people to generate referrals in a structured, professional environment. The central concept of these groups was to have no more than one representative of each business or profession in each of its chapters. Thus, members would not be in competition with one another but would help each other establish and extend word-of-mouth networks throughout the business community.

In *The World's Best Known Marketing Secret,* I laid out a blueprint for building a comprehensive word-of-mouth marketing program that any business, small or large, could use to build sales. As one component of word-of-mouth marketing, I introduced a device for making an immediate, memorable impression on any individual or group you find yourself addressing—a concept I called the *memory hook.*

THE HOOK

HERE'S THE CENTRAL IDEA of the book you're reading now: Who you are, in the eyes of others, depends largely on what they see and hear in the first thirty seconds or so after they meet you. Their first impression of you sets up a bias that colors all their later interactions with you. So the opening moments of your meeting with a new acquaintance often determine whether he or she is interested in listening to your entire message—and a memory hook is something you can use within the first seven seconds to ensure that you will be remembered favorably.

A good memory hook is a brief, memorable self-introduction that engages the other party's interest positively and creates an unbreakable connection between you and your product or service.

A memory hook is simply a brief, memorable self-introduction. The ideal introduction immediately engages the other party's interest positively and creates an unbreakable connection between you and your product or service.

Here's an example of a memory hook. You're a piano tuner and you're introducing yourself to a meeting of local musicians. You say, "I'm Charles J. Woodward, and I run Concert Charley's Piano Tuning Service. If your piano needs fixing, I know which strings to pull."

One of your listeners, Beth, later finds herself talking with Hank, the director of a local recording studio. Hank's regular piano tuner can't seem to make his piano sound right. Beth tells Hank, "Check out Concert Charley—he really knows how to pull strings." You get the job, and your good work at the recording studio soon gets you referrals to other jobs.

From that single, short introduction, and without expensive ad campaigns, your business multiplies. That's word of mouth. And why does Beth remember you? Because you have a memory hook: you're "Concert Charley" and you "pull strings."

This simple notion is so valuable that many people have asked me to elaborate on it. So that I could compile a more comprehensive collection of memory hooks, I began asking people to tell me how they introduced themselves. I got nearly two thousand responses by the time I began writing this book.

THE BOOK

THIS BOOK IS ABOUT MEMORABLE INTRODUCTIONS—how they work, how others have used them, and how to come up with one of your own.

Part I describes how, although life and the marketplace have changed, the desire for personal referrals and recommendations is still with us. It shows how increased competition on regional, national, and global scales has intensified the need for businesses to stand out on a personal or local level. It looks at the emergence of relationship marketing, the proliferation of networking activities, and the importance of word of mouth. It reviews the nature of and differences between personal and group introductions and describes how the first impression you make affects the results of personal contacts, networking, and word-of-mouth marketing. The final chapter of part I describes the principles behind creating and using a memory hook in your business or profession.

In part II you will find a compilation of introductions and memory hooks from business professionals all over North America. To demonstrate how people use expertise, imagination, and humor to describe their businesses, these marketing tools are categorized by form and style: hooks based on your company or personal name or your profession; hooks that are rhymes, puns, or songs; hooks that emphasize quality or excellence; and others. You'll see how some business professionals use memory hooks in their marketing materials, business cards, and stationery. You'll read in their own words how their memory hooks were conceived and how effective they have been in attracting attention and generating business. To give you as many examples as possible of how different businesses and professions use memory hooks, I've concluded each of these chapters with a list of other memory hooks that fit the theme.

Part III has worksheets that will help you develop your own introductions and memory hooks, an index of memory hooks by profession, and—most important!—a form you can use to send me your own memory hook for future editions of this book.

Chapter

2

The More Things
Change . . .

Why We Resist Mass Marketing
and Embrace Word of Mouth

WHAT'S DIFFERENT ABOUT THESE TIMES? There's something
going on in our changing society that makes us want to
reach out and contact others, to form self-help groups, political
action committees, and networking associations. Have our interests and concerns changed? Don't the old ways work any more?

THAT WAS THEN . . .

WHETHER WE ARE SELLERS OR BUYERS—and all of us are both, of course—word of mouth has always been our tool of choice. Until a few decades ago, as consumers we knew our local merchants and tradespeople, and we knew our neighbors, who knew others. Products and services were fewer and harder to find. When we needed to locate a particular product or service, we asked around. One of our friends or acquaintances usually had the answer or knew someone who knew someone who knew. That's what we were comfortable with—a chain of referrals—and it's still the way many of us choose our doctors, dentists, lawyers, and others into whose hands we entrust our most precious assets.

> *Whether we are sellers or buyers, word of mouth has always been our tool of choice.*

As a provider of a product or service, we knew that the chain of referrals worked both ways. If we were good at what we did, word would get around, and we would find ourselves being recommended by our customers to other customers. Because we lived in small towns, we knew many of our customers personally and we knew what our clientele needed and wanted. We could specialize or generalize intelligently: as lawyers, we knew most of our clients needed help with wills, property deeds, and inheritances; as pharmacists, we knew how much of each kind of medicine we would likely dispense. And we knew that taking personal care to deliver the goods and services would almost automatically bring us more business.

. . . AND THIS IS NOW

LIFE AND THE MARKETPLACE ARE DIFFERENT NOW. We live in large cities and commute miles to work and to shop; we live next door to people we barely know who also work in other neighborhoods. In buying and selling most products and services, we've grown accustomed to dealing with strangers. We shop for groceries, medicine, auto parts, and household goods in regional or national chain stores whose economies of scale offer wide selections at low prices. We draw our cash from automatic teller machines. We fill our own cars with gasoline from credit card–activated pumps and drive to other cities to shop in factory outlet malls. We put up with the indignities of self-service "services" and discount houses where salespeople seem to have other things to do, and when we get tired of driving around and being ignored, we shop by mail.

Yet in this era of withdrawing into our cocoons and living by remote control, we still want information. We want to know where our friends found that terrific bed set, who did their taxes, which doctor treats their children. As always, we feel more comfortable doing business with people who have been recommended to us by others.

But do we trust those strangers who moved in next door two months ago and will probably be gone next year? Do we trust the stock clerk at Humongous Foods, who's working there between classes at taxidermy school, to tell us which can of tomato sauce has the least iodine? Can we even get someone to talk to us at Clem's Club, where we need a forklift to haul our giant, economy-size box of detergent to our Suburban?

These days, we have to work harder to find people with whom we share interests.

No, we want guidance from a reliable source—a friend, a family member, someone with whom we have something in common. These days, we have to work harder to find people with whom we share interests. This is the reason behind the growing phenomenon of networking.

HIGH WIRE WITH A NET

NETWORKING, IN OUR GLOBAL VILLAGE, takes the place of the small community of various interests we grew up in. Instead of seeking the advice of neighbors we don't know to aid our search for goods, services, information, and entertainment we can no longer find just down the block, we join consumers' unions, support groups, and media networks to gain access to those things across the state, the nation, the world. And in joining them, we get back some of the feeling of security that we lost when we left the small town and moved to the city.

You may wonder why we should feel so isolated when it's getting easier every day to communicate. We can pick up the phone in our home, office, back yard, or automobile and dial up practically anybody, practically anywhere. We can watch events unfolding in real time on the other side of the planet. We can send and receive e-mail more quickly and cheaply than mailing a stamped letter. John Naisbitt, in *Megatrends*, suspects that we are "matching each new technology with a compensatory human response." According to this argument, the more we communicate long distance, "the more people will aggregate [and] want to be with other people."[1] The rapid growth of networking would appear to support this idea. Of course, you could also reason that both networking and the proliferation of online communication are a response to our increasing isolation.

> **Why do we feel so isolated when it's getting easier every day to communicate?**

INFORMATION, PLEASE

MOST BUSINESSES HAVE TRIED TO COMPENSATE for their size and the loss of personal contact by advertising in the mass media. Today's consumer is targeted each day by some two thousand advertising, marketing, and public relations messages via radio, television, billboards, mail, magazines, and newspapers (and now opening at a computer near you, the Internet).[2] Many of these are never seen or heard; few get more than a passing glance. We have become skilled at hitting the "mute" button.

If you're selling, offering, or providing a product or service—whether you're working for someone else or running your own business—you know what a challenge it is to make yourself known in such an ad-saturated market. To reach your target audience, your marketing campaign must break through this barrage. You have to stand out.

Let's suppose you decide to devote your entire marketing budget to large-scale advertising. Even if your campaign brings your product or service to the prospect's attention, that alone seldom closes the sale (unless you're selling something the buyer is looking for, such as a particular food item). As most experienced marketing people know, someone must still call on the prospect and convert him into a paying client.[3] This costs, on the average, nearly $200 per sales call.[4]

Thus, in the end, despite all your marketing and advertising efforts, making the sale often comes down to making a good impression on the prospect in a face-to-face encounter. An Organizational Development Institute study found that none of the traditional methods—direct mail, trade publication ads, telephone marketing, newspaper ads, billboards—were nearly as effective as in-person strategies.[5] In his best seller *Thriving on Chaos,* Tom Peters recommends devoting 75 percent of your marketing dollars and energy to establishing and maintaining a word-of-mouth network.[6]

Tom Peters recommends devoting 75 percent of your marketing dollars and energy to establishing and maintaining a word-of-mouth network.

It's especially frustrating to me that our colleges and universities are teaching the next generation of business professionals not about word-of-mouth marketing but about creating and managing multi-million-dollar advertising campaigns.[7] For every graduate who becomes the marketing director of a Fortune 500 company, thousands will go to work for small businesses, where almost all the new jobs are being created, or as account executives, not marketing supervisors, in larger companies.[8] Most will be thrown into the field to sell the company's products or services firsthand.[9]

THE BOOM IN BUSINESS NETWORKING

JUST AS NETWORKING IS SOCIETY'S REACTION to personal cocooning, the business networking phenomenon is, in my view, a compensatory response to the proliferation of high-tech workplaces that reduce in-person interaction. In our businessperson roles we have grown just as isolated as we have in our suburb-dweller roles. We don't know many of the professionals in our community, so we jump at the chance to meet and talk with others in the same room, and we soon learn the built-in benefits of business networking.

Some would counter, "What about networking on the World Wide Web? We don't need to actually meet people to do business." I don't deny this; I've made great contacts on the Web. Yet we know instinctively, and some of us are old enough to remember, that there are some things that you can experience better by meeting people face to face.[10]

There's more behind the growth of business networking than just our reaction to high-tech isolation, however. We are now familiar with a well-established corporate trend toward downsizing. In a fast-changing, globally competitive environment, big companies often react too slowly, allowing upstart companies to capture prime segments of their markets. This is why big corporations are divesting divisions, laying off employees, and cutting advertising budgets.

As companies get smaller and more efficient and spend less on mass marketing, they become more aware of the need for and advantages of seeking new customers by networking and closing the sale in person. Organizational development consultants, in particular, have found making contacts through a third-party "matchmaker" to be their most effective marketing approach.[11] Developing referral business and word-of-mouth marketing have become conscious marketing strategies for companies both large and small, but the newer breed of small businesses in particular depend on multiple strategic alliances with other businesses.

Before I founded Business Network Int'l. (BNI) in 1985, business referral groups were few and far between. Today they cover North America coast to coast and are spreading fast overseas.[12] According to the *Directory of Networking Organizations,* many businesses develop 50 to 90 percent of their client base through networking and the referrals it generates.[13]

GETTING THE WORD OUT

AS I DEMONSTRATED in *The World's Best Known Marketing Secret,* the key to successful business networking is word of mouth—the knack of getting other people to spread the word on your behalf. Most business people understand this; they know it instinctively. But what is less obvious to them these days is how to accomplish it. As Regis McKenna, author of *The Regis Touch,* says, "Word of mouth is probably the most powerful form of communication in the business world. . . . [It is] so obvious a communications medium that most people do not take the time to analyze or understand its structure."

> *Word-of-mouth marketing is more about farming than about hunting.*

As a way to cultivate business, word of mouth is as powerful as ever. But the environment has changed enormously since the days when the town had two plumbers and one Chevy dealer and everybody knew everybody. In this age of mass-media overkill, what's difficult is to stand out from the competition—to be remembered.

A pivotal idea in *The World's Best Known Marketing Secret* is that word-of-mouth marketing is more about farming than about hunting. Your effort should be concentrated on cultivating relationships for referrals and repeat business, not on continually hunting for new contacts. This is more true today than ever, because it's easy to lose referrals to the next competitor who gets the prospect's attention. It's important to be remembered, to stick in the prospect's mind like a song that won't go away.

MAKING YOURSELF MEMORABLE

THERE ARE TWO KEY ELEMENTS in distinguishing yourself from the crowd of competitors. The first is to build and maintain a reputation for good work and integrity that becomes a topic of conversation when people talk about you. The reason word of mouth is so effective is that people naturally trust their friends and colleagues more than strangers. When someone whose judgment you respect says, "She's the best interior designer in town," it means much more than the same message brought to you by a newspaper, television, or billboard ad.

The other key element is to make it as easy as possible for people to remember your name—and that's what this book is about. In the next chapter we will explore the point in space and time where you start to become memorable: the introduction.

Chapter
3

The Art of the Introduction

How to Meet Prospects Individually and in Groups

I NTRODUCING YOURSELF IS A NECESSARY PART of effective
networking in most situations, networking events, business
meetings, service organizations, and social situations. It's useful
to think in terms of two kinds of self-introductions: person-to-
person and person-to-group. When you're attending a meeting or

any event where your goal is to network, you will often have the opportunity to use both.

A networking event is in some ways like a purely social gathering, and in other ways quite different. At both, your immediate goal is to learn, in a short time, as much as possible about other people while providing carefully selected bits of information about yourself. At a social event, the information exchanged is mostly personal, and you may wish to concentrate on a few individuals—perhaps even one special person. In a networking event, however, the information is business related, and you wish to make contact with as many people as you can in a time that is probably very limited. When you are networking with others and telling them about what you do, your underlying hope is that they will use your services and pass the message to others who will also use your services and in turn keep spreading your message.

FIRST IMPRESSIONS

THE FIRST THIRTY SECONDS is the most important part of the entire process.[1] The first impression you make on another person is usually the one that sticks. As Norman King has noted, "Any extreme type of behavior . . . sets up a bias for all your subsequent perceptions of the person to whom you are talking. . . . First perceptions tend to be most lasting and are difficult to shake up and change."[2]

> *The first impression you make on another person is usually the one that sticks.*

Meeting people is not really the first thing you do when you walk into a gathering. Before you open your mouth, before you shake your first hand, you have already started communicating information about yourself to everyone present. Do you seem pleased to be there, eager to make friends? Do you slouch into the room as the counterculture's answer to middle-class complacency? Do your attitude, your posture, and your expression shout, "Here I am; come kiss my ring"?

Introducing yourself begins long before you arrive. Check with colleagues or friends on appropriate attire. If you've been putting off getting a haircut, now's the time. Load up with business cards and brochures, and bring a pocket notebook for taking down names, addresses, and phone numbers. Make sure your car is gassed up. Arrive on time, not in haste or panic. Be yourself, but be prepared to respect the sensibilities of your hosts. Remember, the first message you communicate is *you*.

MEETING AN INDIVIDUAL

WHEN YOU INTRODUCE YOURSELF, or are introduced, to another person at a networking event, you are limited by time and attention span. Your goal is to have high-quality interactions with as many people as possible. You don't want to appear rushed, of course—that can come across as rudeness—but at the same time you don't want to overstay your welcome. As Milo Frank points out, the average attention span is about half a minute.[3]

The best way to overcome first-meeting jitters is to practice.

Take seven to ten seconds to introduce yourself, concentrating not so much on who you are as on what you do.[4] You can't tell anyone much about who you are in a few seconds—and you don't need to.[5] What you really need to convey is what you do, because that's what you're selling. At the same time, you can usually communicate a lot of basic information about yourself in the way you relate to your contact—your tone of voice, your handshake, your posture. Make eye contact, smile, and speak clearly. It's important to be relaxed and natural. If you're obviously nervous, it will distract from what you say and make the other person nervous.

The best way to overcome first-meeting jitters is to practice. Take the time to plan your introduction and prepare some concise and descriptive overviews of your products or services. Rehearse what you want to say about yourself until you can repeat it almost unconsciously. Then, when you meet someone for the first time, you can give that person a good explanation of what you have to offer.

Most professionals who are skilled at meeting and presenting themselves to other individuals and groups know that the best way to sound natural is to practice, practice, practice. It sounds paradoxical, but it's true: the better rehearsed you are, the more natural you'll appear. That's because knowing exactly what you want to say will give you confidence, and confidence will let you be natural. If you are unsure of your message, you're more likely to stutter and stammer and flail around for something to talk about. If you know what you want to talk about before going in, however, you can relax and enjoy the give-and-take of conversation.

> *Refine your introduction until it is a natural expression of yourself that fits the situation.*

Set up imaginary meetings in your mind; think of particular questions you might be asked about yourself or your business; rehearse how you would answer. Refine your self-introduction until it is a natural expression of yourself that fits the situation. Practice different approaches until you find the words that best represent you while getting your message across so that people will remember you.[6] Practice two or three sentences that sum up, as colorfully and succinctly as possible, what you do. Often the most colorful and succinct thing you can say is your memory hook.

It's also important (and helpful in keeping your composure) to remember that the other person is often in the same situation as you—wishing to meet people, to make new contacts, perhaps unfamiliar with others at the event and unsure about how to get started. Make it easy on the other person and on yourself; assume you have some interests in common. It's an opportunity for you both that may lead to greater things—a chance for discovery, not disaster.[7]

Now—how do you get the conversation going? Try to begin naturally, just as you would a casual conversation with nothing riding on it. If you are too worried about what to say, you may appear hesitant or standoffish. As Susan RoAne reminds us, "Too often we lose an opportunity to meet someone because we spend precious time trying to think of the perfect opening line."[8]

A good way to start is to keep it simple. Say something that will project your personality or your profession and at the same time invite a response. Think of something you have in common with the other person—you work in the same office building, for example, or live in the same city, or shop at the same store. Of course, one thing you know you have in common is that you're at the same event:[9]

> *Say something that will project your personality and invite a response.*

▼ "What a beautiful facility for a banquet!"

▼ "How did you get involved with the . . . Club?"

▼ "I hear the speaker for today is an expert on . . ."

▼ "Can you tell me a little bit about this organization?"

▼ "This is my first time to attend a . . . meeting."

▼ "Is this your first time here? Let me introduce you to . . ."

▼ "I'm looking for. . . . Can you help me?"

Once you've broken the ice, try to find out more about the other person's business or interests. In a networking group like BNI, you are probably the only person there in your business specialty; therefore, you can't assume that anyone you haven't met knows a lot about your business. Nor is it likely that you will know everything about the other person's field. Ask questions that indicate a genuine interest but are not intrusive:

▼ "How did you get your start?"

▼ "What do you enjoy most about your work?"

▼ "What do you do differently from others in your line of work?"

▼ "What trends do you see in your business?"

▼ "What have you found to be the most effective way to promote your business?"[10]

By showing an interest in the other person's work, you are accomplishing several things. You are (1) cultivating a friendship, (2) gaining potentially valuable information, and (3) inviting the other person to ask you questions about *your* business. It is not being hypocritical to recognize that everyone has self-interest foremost in mind. To the extent that those interests coincide, you are helping yourself by being helpful to the other person. As Cutlip, Center, and Broom point out in *Effective Public Relations*, "Events, words, or any other stimuli affect opinion only insofar as their relationship to self-interest is apparent."[11]

> It is not being hypocritical to recognize that everyone has self-interest foremost in mind.

When you tell the other person who you are and what you do, be ready with your memory hook. Keep in mind, however, that not all memory hooks are equally appropriate in casual conversation. One that's humorous, such as a pun or a funny couplet of doggerel, can work especially well at this juncture. However, a longer memory hook, such as a jingle, or one that is more serious or educational, may be awkward in a face-to-face discussion. Use your judgment.

Finally, here's another time factor to remember when meeting an individual, according to Norman King: "By the time the second hand has traveled five times around your wristwatch, two things will have happened: You will have decided exactly how much you trust or distrust your [new] business acquaintance, and the other person will have decided exactly how much he or she trusts or distrusts you."[12]

So don't overstay your welcome; serious networkers, recognizing that they have limited time to introduce themselves and convey the essence of what they do, generally avoid lengthy small talk. At most gatherings, your objective of cultivating contacts must be balanced against meeting as many contacts as possible. Excuse yourself as gracefully as possible from the conversation—for instance, by introducing your new friend to someone else—and move on.

MEETING A GROUP

WHEN YOU MEET AN INDIVIDUAL, your conversation will be somewhat free form; you can go in knowing what message you want to convey, but you must respond appropriately to the other person's remarks or you will seem canned and artificial—or worse, stupid. Standing up in front of a group, however, you'll be the one doing all the talking—at least for a while.

With a group, you can assume you will have their attention for a few minutes and be able to convey your message uninterrupted. But your time is still limited. Audiences quickly turn their attention elsewhere if you don't grab it and keep it right at the start. People in a group sitting ten feet or more away from you don't feel the need to be as polite as an individual standing in your face. If you bore them, you'll quickly find yourself speaking to nodding heads or drowned out by private conversations.

This is why a presentation to a group is something you especially need to prepare for. You'll have more freedom to plan your remarks and to practice them so that you can sound natural. But you'll also have to be more entertaining to keep their attention and ensure that they remember you. This, again, is a good place for a memory hook: right up front. And since you can prepare your remarks in advance, you'll find it easier to fit your memory hook, whatever its form, into an appropriate context. If you set them up for it, you can sing the whole opera.

Some networking organizations have all their members stand at each meeting and, in round-robin fashion, give a one-minute overview to the entire group. If you're a member of a group like this, it is vitally important to vary your presentations. In fact, I would urge you to develop and rehearse several scripts to use when attending networking meetings. One of your scripts should to be an overview of what you do. Other presentations can address various aspects of your product or service.

On page 153 of this book you will find a worksheet titled "Anatomy of a 60-Second Presentation." This outline will help you assemble the information you need to present yourself and your business effectively to a networking group. The same information can be assembled in other ways, in different proportions and lengths and with different details, when you are to address other kinds of meetings or groups. In general, this information includes

▼ Your name

▼ Your business or profession

▼ Your memory hook

▼ A brief description of your business or profession

▼ A benefit statement of one particular product or service you offer (what you do that helps others)

Your name and your business or profession are easy enough. A memory hook, a brief description, and a benefit statement can be separate items, but more often they are intertwined in your message. For example, it's easy to mention your business along with the benefits of your product or service. I suggest telling people what you do, as well as what you are:

▼ "I'm a financial planner and I help people plan for their future."

▼ "I'm an advertising and marketing consultant and I help companies get the most out of their advertising dollar."

These explanations are more effective than saying, "I do financial planning," or "I plan advertising campaigns."

Many people who are in business groups that meet every week have a tendency to say the same old thing, time after time. If you do this, many people will tune you out when you speak, because they've already heard your message several times. Your best bet is to give a brief overview, then concentrate on just one element of your business for the remaining part of your presentation.

The competition in word-of-mouth marketing is the same as competition in the larger world: you compete for the prospect's perception of what you sell. Your prospect devotes a limited part of his or her memory to competing products. Your best chance of keeping a part of that memory for yourself is to focus the prospect's attention on a particular aspect of what you do. You're more memorable if you're known for selling yard eggs than if you're just another farmer.[13]

Here's a key point to remember. In a true business-networking organization such as BNI, the fact that among those present you are probably the most knowledgable person in your field gives you an automatic authority that is invaluable in selling your message. The members of your audience are there to network their own services and, at the same time, to learn; they are receptive and willing to consider opinions from an authoritative source—you.[14]

Keep your message simple, direct, and high-impact.

And here's the key to a memorable introduction: Keep your message simple, direct, and high-impact. There's a story that's often recounted about Calvin Coolidge, one of the most taciturn people ever to become a public figure. A reporter once told him she had bet her colleagues that she could get him to say more than two words. "You lose," said Coolidge.[15]

The strongest impression is the one you can make in the shortest time; that's why a memory hook is the best approach.

4

How to Make a Memory Hook

A Mix-and-Match Guide to the Key Ingredients

WHETHER YOU REALIZE IT OR NOT, you already know a lot about memory hooks. You've been using them, consciously or unconsciously, since you were small. When you were in the third grade, what was your best friend's nickname? Where were you living when "MacArthur Park" was playing on the radio?

Who do you think of whenever you someone say, "Ehhh—what's up, Doc?"? Mere fragments of phrases, jokes, songs, and rhymes remind us of people, places, and events we have not seen or experienced in years—and they stay with us all our lives.

How Memory Hooks Are Born

The basic principle is simple. Suppose your name is Montmorency Terwilliger Veerhogen and you own a television repair shop. At a party, your friend introduces you around the room as his favorite TV repairman. To the first half-dozen people he says, "I'd like you to meet Montmorency Terwilliger Veerhogen." Then he tires of repeating your enormous name and begins introducing you as just "Monty." Suddenly, out of nowhere, an idea strikes him as amusing. You become "MTV, the best video man in town."

It is often another person who discovers the memory hook for you; you may be too accustomed to your name and your business to make the connection.

At the end of the evening, you discover that few of the people you were first introduced to remember your name or what you do, though some call you "Monty." But of those to whom you are "MTV," all promise to send you their electronics for repair. Does this give you any ideas for a good business name?

This is an example of one way a memory hook can be created—by accident or serendipity. Oddly enough, it is often another person who discovers the memory hook for you; you may be too accustomed to your name and your business to make the connection. But if you sit around waiting for someone else to create your memory hook, you may end up waiting a long time. Here's a better plan: Invest some business time in a search for a memory hook. Ask friends, partners, associates, even friendly competitors to help.

Sometimes your name itself becomes the key to being remembered; sometimes it's your business name. Or perhaps you can come up with an apt two-line rhyming ditty, or a pun on your business name or profession, or perhaps just a succinct, pithy way of describing what you do. It doesn't really matter what you use; as long as people find it easy to remember, it's a good memory hook.

You may have heard the term "tag line," another way of saying "memory hook." As defined by Lynne Waymon and Anne Baber, a tag line is "an additional comment that gives more information than just your name. It's an identifier that puts you 'in context.'" A tag line is a provocative, energetic way of describing what you do. John Muir, the famous 19th-century naturalist, often introduced himself by saying, "I study the inventions of God."[1] This was far more memorable than saying, "I am a botanist, a glaciologist, and a conservationist."

WHAT MAKES A GOOD MEMORY HOOK?

THE KEY WORD IN "MEMORY HOOK" IS "MEMORY." If it's going to work the way you want it to, to pop into the prospect's mind whenever the need for your product or service arises, it has to be easy to remember. The best way to make it memorable is to make it vivid and short.

Short's not hard to figure out; one snappy phrase or short sentence is all you need. Anything more not only is wasted, it can also get in the way. Which is easier to remember: "The items available for purchase during our special sale are the ones that are on display beneath this sign," or "What you see is what you get"?

SEE IT, HEAR IT, FEEL IT

A good memory hook often appeals to the basic senses—sight, hearing, taste, smell, touch. When meeting people in person or presenting your product or service using marketing materials, you should invoke the senses as strongly as possible—in a pleasurable way, of course.[2] You will see many good examples of this principle in part II of this book, but here are some to show you what I mean:

"For balloons with a flair, remember the bear in the air." This memory hook, for a retail seller of toy balloons, grabs the visual imagination and paints an image that sticks in the mind. The next time a prospect discovers a need for balloons—for a party, a wedding, a convention—she may well find the image of the "bear in the air" popping into her mind. Or she may be driving down the street and see the balloon shop's big bear sign and think, "Oh, yeah, I need to remember this place next month when I start decorating the gym for the class reunion."

A Tennessee floor care company creates a vivid visual with this slogan: "We make your floors reflect well on you."

A good memory hook often appeals to the basic senses—sight, hearing, taste, smell, touch.

Here's a memory hook, used by a travel agency, that conjures up the memory of a popular song: "Come fly away with me." Most people of a certain age will be reminded of Sinatra's hit of several decades back. With the exception of smells, nothing cranks up a pleasure trip into nostalgia like the fond memory of an old song.

How do you conjure up the sensation of touch in a slogan? Here's one way: "If you want to get rubbed the right way, see Jim." This is how one inventive massage technician attracts business. And any Dallasite who hears "Sweat's my name, air conditioning's my game" will probably feel a shiver of dread thinking of that hot August day last year when the fan stopped working, and call air conditioning specialist Tim Sweat.

MAKE 'EM LAUGH, MAKE 'EM CRY

Another "sense" that is often invoked in the best memory hooks may be the most important one of all: the sense of humor. When you want to catch and hold someone's attention, tickling his funny bone is perhaps the surest way of being remembered. In fact, one thing that most of the memory hooks in this book have in common is that they are funny. Making people laugh is one of the fastest ways of breaking down the barriers between strangers and of winning the prospect's good will.

Two of the examples that you've just read are puns, a form of humor that everyone groans at but tries to remember to pass along. The power of the pun comes from the element of surprise; your listener (or reader) thinks you're saying one thing but suddenly discovers that you're saying something else because you've either distorted the word or defined it another way. Here are some other examples of memory hooks that use puns or word play:

> *Making people laugh is one of the fastest ways of breaking down the barriers between strangers and of winning the prospect's good will.*

▼ "We check your shorts," an electrician offers.

▼ "We're dyeing to save you money," says a company that can change the color of your carpet.

▼ "Be true to your teeth or they will be false to you," warns an Ohio dentist.

For pure name recognition, some of the most effective puns are made on a company's or person's name:

▼ Bob Howe, a mortgage lender in Irvine, California, says, "Know Howe to get your next loan!"

▼ The people at Truecolor Screen Print & Graphics of Vernon, Connecticut, use their company name in their invitation: "Let us help you show your true colors."

On the other hand, a memory hook doesn't have to be funny to be memorable. Sometimes you just need to reach out and pluck someone's heartstrings. Here's a good example that I once heard from a real estate salesperson whose name sadly I cannot remember: "I help people find a home. Not a house, but a home; not a place where they just live, but a place where they love to live."

VERSE—OR WORSE

Using verse is a sure way to catch someone's interest. Before most people could read, storytellers passed down tribal legends in verse form to make them easier to remember. The tradition lingers. Most people can recite from memory poetry or doggerel or humorous verse, whether sonnets or limericks, and anyone who can read is instinctively attracted to words that rhyme.

Before most people could read, storytellers passed down tribal legends in verse form to make them easier to remember.

If you can use your name as part of the rhyme, so much the better. Here are some examples:

▼ "When things go blurry, don't stop to 'ponda'; stumble to 17th Street and see Dr. Honda" (an optometrist).

▼ If you find yourself in trouble with the authorities, perhaps the following poem, penned by a lawyer in Portland, Maine, will spring to mind: "When the cops are in the foyer, call Marchese, your friendly lawyer."

PIRACY OR PARODY?

Many of the memory hooks you will read later work because they take a familiar saying and rephrase it, usually with humor—that is, they parody a song or a phrase the reader or listener will recognize. But you have to be careful; some authors, especially songwriters, are quite militant about copyright infringement.

▼ "When you're in a commotion, who're you gonna call? Law in motion!" proclaims paralegal Gloria Jones of Long Beach, California. It's a good bet she's seen *Ghostbusters*.

▼ Thomas Quirk, a banker in White Plains, New York, offers this thought, perhaps borrowed from a farewell speech by a famous WWII general: "Old bankers never die—they just lose interest!"

▼ And here's one that the borrower, Glendale, California, dentist Joe Wilson, can never be sued for: "I believe in the tooth, the whole tooth, and nothing but the tooth, so help me God."

THE OLD DOUBLE REVERSE

One of the most powerful language devices is a statement in which the second part either rephrases or reverses the first. The original meaning may be reinforced, slightly altered, or turned around entirely, leading to intriguing mental juxtapositions. For instance:

▼ "A business without a sign is a sign of no business" (a sign company in Canyon Springs, California).

▼ "If your hair is not becoming to you, then you should be coming to me" (a hair stylist in Covina, California).

▼ "A roof done right is water-tight, but a roof done wrong won't last too long" (verse by Ken McCarthy of Anaheim, California).

▼ "I take care of your computer so you can take care of your business" (a computer consultant in Glenwood Springs, Colorado).

These approaches should give you an idea of some of the tools and resources you can use to construct your own memory hook. Notice that many memory hooks use a combination of these techniques. Almost anything you do in the line of word play will come out funny—and that's the way it should be, unless you'd rather appeal to the heart. Song lyrics usually rhyme, so if you parody a song, it should rhyme as well. And any of these techniques can be more effective if your memory hook is short and snappy and appeals to the senses.

WHEN AND HOW TO USE A MEMORY HOOK

THE BEST MEMORY HOOK is one that you can use in many contexts. It should work in a pure word-of-mouth setting, as when you are attending a meeting of a networking group. It should work on your business card, on your letterhead, your calendars, your giveaway pens (another reason to keep it short), even your print ads and—at the top of the expense scale—your broadcast ads. Whether it's mass advertising or face-to-face, you want people to think of you, and you alone, when they see, hear, or remember your memory hook.

We've already talked about the least expensive way to use a memory hook: to introduce yourself to another person or to a group. This will cost you nothing but your time, a few business cards, and perhaps a membership fee if you join the group. Introducing yourself to others carries an additional advantage: you can expand on your memory hook. You can go beyond the single phrase or sentence or bit of verse and add a few significant details.

At one networking meeting I attended, a security systems consultant gave us a memorable commercial. He stood before us, turned his steely gaze on us, and said nothing for a moment. The room fell silent, and everyone's attention focused on him. Then he boomed, "I have a criminal mind! If you use me, I'll try to break into your house. By doing so, I'll be able to show you how a real criminal can get into your house in a matter of minutes. But more importantly, I'll be able to show you how to stop him!" No one who was there soon forgot the impression he made.

At another meeting, the portly owner of a popular Italian restaurant stood up and exclaimed, "As you can see, I'm a walking billboard for our pasta!" He went on to describe in mouth-watering detail how his restaurant used only the finest cheeses, handmade pasta, and a wonderful slow-cooked sauce made from the freshest ingredients. His presentation worked on our must vulnerable senses: taste and smell. By the time he was finished, we were all ready to adjourn to his restaurant.

Part

II

Memory Hook Themes

*A Potpourri of Ways
to Hook Your Prospect*

PART II

CHAPTER 5
Draw Attention to Your Name

▼

CHAPTER 6
Highlight Your Company Name

▼

CHAPTER 7
Communicate Your Profession

▼

CHAPTER 8
Tell Them Quality Is Important to You

▼

CHAPTER 9
Educate As You Sell

▼

CHAPTER 10
Rhyme It or Sing It

▼

CHAPTER 11
Play with the Words

▼

CHAPTER 12
Take the Next Step

C h a p t e r

5

Draw Attention to Your Name

*Getting Them to Remember
Who You Are*

IT'S NOT ENOUGH SIMPLY TO BE REMEMBERED; what's really important is that your *name* be remembered. It does you little good to entertain your prospects if, weeks later and in need of your services, they wonder, "Who was that funny lady who caters kids' birthday parties?" Name recall is vital!

People who attend networking events understand better than most how important it is for people to remember their name. That's why the art of introducing yourself to other individuals and to the group is an art worth cultivating. Once people know your name and your business, you may think you have communicated all you need to communicate. But you can go a step further and make it easy for them: you can use your personal name in your memory hook.

Even major advertisers know the importance of a personal name, whether real or fictional. Most people chuckle at the memory of "Bartles" and "James" selling wine coolers on the front porch and know that folksy, down-to-earth Dave Thomas is the founder of Wendy's. When you're networking, selling one-to-one via word of mouth, your personal name can be an even greater asset than your brand name. If your name is in your memory hook and it's a memorable memory hook, you're guaranteed name recall. Many small-business owners have discovered compelling ways to use their names, as the following examples show.

"When you're Awesome, you can't go wrong."

"We're Awesome Computer Service and we strive to live up to our name."

Vandar and Zena Awesome
Awesome Computer Service
Moreno Valley, CA

I [Zena] kept my maiden name when we got married. We planned on changing both our names some time in the future. After almost seven years of marriage, it seemed to be the right time. We tossed around a lot of names. One of the requirements was being at the beginning of the alphabet, something new for both of us. We wanted a name that was fun and easy to remember. It was obvious that Awesome Computer Service would be a perfect name for our business.

Of all the memory hooks using a person's name that I've heard over the years, this is the only one where people actually changed their names to create one—especially one that would appear early in the Yellow Pages listings. You have to admit, it will take a while for you to forget Awesome Computer Service.

"Young or old . . . see Nold."

> *Larry Nold*
> *MassMutual Insurance & Financial Services*
> *Findlay, OH*

My dad had an auto repair business for 29 years and he used this memory hook: "New or old . . . see Nold." Some years after Dad died and I went into the life insurance and financial services industry selling products for MassMutual, I felt I needed a memory hook that was easy to remember. What better memory hook than "Young or old . . . see Nold," along with the follow-up, "I help people plan their financial future." It stuck, and I've used it ever since.

I really like Larry's memory hook because it carries on a tradition that started with his dad. Not only is there something special about that connection, it also utilizes a phrase that is recognized throughout a good segment of the community.

LARRY NOLD

SEYMOUR & ASSOCIATES

MassMutual

Young or Old See Nold

Findlay Office
1265 Fostoria Avenue
Findlay, Ohio 45840
Phone: (419) 424-1626

Toledo Office
1789 Indian Wood Circle
Suite 200
Maumee, Ohio 43537
Phone: (419) 893-9759

Pass on to Friends!

"Don't Gamble with Your Real Estate Needs— Call the Wright Realtor Today!"

Roberta Wright
Realtor
Century 21 Champions
Beaverton, OR

In real estate you want the right house, in the right area, at the right price, with the right amenities. Who better to work with than "the Wright Realtor" to make all this happen? I also knew that a home is usually the largest purchase people make, and it's nothing to gamble with, so on the back of my business card I put the queen of diamonds with my face, stating, "Don't gamble with your real estate needs—call the Wright Realtor today!" I've had people tell me this is the best and most professional card they've ever seen. My card gives everyone the opportunity to chuckle and at the same time remember what I do and what my name is.

I also back up my memory hook on my voice mail and pager and all my fliers and advertising. My voice mail message says, "Hi, this is Roberta Wright, the Wright Realtor. I'm sorry I can't take your call, but I'm out doing all the Wright things. "

In her quest for something to set her apart from her competition, Roberta has obviously come up with a very effective memory hook. Notice how many ways she uses it: on her card, in her marketing materials, and—most interestingly—on her voice mail. This is a very creative way to get people to remember you.

"You Can Expect to Get More with Les."

Les Harris
Realtor
Century 21—Yarrow & Associates
Palmdale, CA

When I first decided on my memory hook, I was newly retired as a manager with Pacific Bell. I was entering the field of real estate in an area where there were more than twelve hundred other Realtors. I believed people would trust me to help them once they knew how I would deal with them, but the problem seemed to be how to get them to call me and to remember me.

It hit me that everyone wants to get a deal. I thought of "Get more with Les," but that didn't seem to say what I wanted it to. So I changed it to "Expect to get more with Les." I wanted to provide exemplary service to truly meet the needs, wants, and desires of my clients. I wanted my clients to have expectations about what I could do for them. And I now find it prompts me to have expectations for myself. I put it on everything I do. So "Expect to get more with Les" means you can expect to get more service, and that translates to a better deal.

Les Harris's memory hook works on two levels: he uses it to make a pun, a sure way to get people to remember; and people like to have a name to ask for when contacting a company for a service.

Here are several other good examples of how to use your name to make a memory connection for the buyer. Note the use of puns and rhymes; these folks don't mind engaging in a little horseplay with their names to make their pitch.

51

"See Nichols for dollars."

John Nichols
Financial services
Indianapolis, IN

"Know Howe to get your next loan!"

Bob Howe
Mortgage lender
Irvine, CA

"Sweat's my name; air conditioning's my game."

Tim Sweat
Air/heat specialist
Dallas, TX

"When things go blurry, don't stop to 'ponda,' stumble to 17th Street and see Dr. Honda."

Dr. Mel Honda
Optometrist
Santa Ana, CA

"If you want complex legal problems made simple, think Simon."

Marc Simon
Lawyer
Las Vegas, NV

C h a p t e r

6

Highlight Your Company Name

Connecting Who You Are with What You Do

COMMERCIAL ADVERTISING AGENCIES make billions of dollars inventing ad campaigns for large companies selling brand-name products and services. For the most part, according to market research, they succeed in generating name recognition, which is half the battle for making the sale. However, sometimes much of that expensive publicity goes wide of the target. People remember the ad but not the brand name. Here's a pop quiz:

1. Which long-distance company do you think of when you see a straight pin falling?
   a. AT&T
   b. MCI
   c. Sprint
2. Which cleaning product is "stronger than dirt"?
   a. Ajax
   b. Biz
   c. Comet
3. Which coffee is good to the last drop?
   a. Taster's Choice
   b. Maxwell House
   c. Folger's

If you're like most people, you won't remember more than one of these products or services.[1] Without the name, the connection may or may not register on the prospect's memory banks. But nobody forgets "Oh, I'd love to be an Oscar Mayer wiener," because the brand name's in it.

> **"Remember, at Custom Office Furniture, your furniture does not have to be custom—we just make it look that way!"**

Scott Epstein
Custom Office Furniture
Las Vegas, NV

My memory hook conveys Custom Office Furniture's philosophy. Since we deal with several different manufacturers, we can tailor the furniture to suit everyone's needs, from the big corporate office to the small home office, at a competitive price.

A memory hook is particularly effective if it sets a business apart from its competition. In this case, it not only does that, but it also explains that the company does both custom and stock furniture. This is important, because the name of the company implies that it may do only custom work. A good memory hook can educate the listener about some key element of the business that might otherwise be missed because of the limitations of a business name.

> ### "Emerald Carpet Care, the jewel of the carpet cleaners!"

Becky Mays
Emerald Carpet Care
Lancaster, CA

The name Emerald Carpet Care came into being by accident. My husband and his cousin were just sitting around one evening several years ago, thinking up names for companies, even before they started their own businesses. They kicked around a bunch of names of gems and stones, thinking they denoted quality. They rejected "diamond" as being too common, but liked "emerald." So when it came time for us to start our own business, we called it "Emerald Carpet Care."

EMERALD CARPET CARE
The Jewel of the Carpet Cleaners!

COMMERCIAL • RESIDENTIAL

(805) 946-2106 • (800) 305-3275

Norman and Becky Mays   2616 Via Madalena
Owners   Lancaster, CA 93535

Later, when we were trying to think up a nice slogan, my son joked, "The jewel of the carpet cleaners." We liked it so well we decided to use it. At first we used it only on our coupons, but later we started putting it on our business cards, letterhead, and brochures, and even in our closing line on the bottom of our invoices. We also put the emerald, very large, on the back of our work shirts, so people see them around town and on the job.

"If you have a wet basement, it should B-Dry!"

Ralph Jones
B-Dry Systems
Basement waterproofing
Bedford Hills, NY

My first exposure to the term "memory hook" was at my first BNI meeting in White Plains, New York. It was readily apparent that simplicity was the most effective approach. Thus, I decided to use my customers' own words: "I want my basement to be dry." The customer requiring my services obviously has water in his basement. Hence, my hook.

"WDEF Radio: We Design Effective Frequency."

Lisa Meades
Sales
WDEF Radio AM & FM
Chattanooga, TN

WDEF Radio is an example of the creativity I learned in radio and applied to word association for my networking efforts. I don't just sell spots, I create campaigns to fill the client's needs. Every advertiser is different, and some have limited budgets. WDEF Radio can help anyone reach her marketing goals by using Effective Frequency. It is very difficult to explain what I do in sixty seconds at networking meetings, so I felt this would help people understand frequency and reach. That's what makes radio work; each client receives individual packages designed specifically for her needs. In my business, a record month is a big deal. I beat my old record by $6,000. Using this memory hook helped me get there.

> "In Your Face! Name Recognition Specialists. We keep your business name, logo, and phone number in the face of your clients and prospects, so they'll call you instead of your competition!"

Jim Walters
In Your Face!
Advertising specialties
Orlando, FL

I worked for an advertising specialty company for about two and a half years and taught myself the business. When I decided to start my own company, I asked an associate who had been in advertising for over twenty years what to call my business. He asked me what I wanted to do with it. I said, "I want to keep business names, logos, and phone numbers in front of my clients' prospects. My associate replied, "In Your Face!" I laughed and said, "It's perfect!" We then decided to add the definitive tag line under the company name: "Name Recognition Specialists."

It has been phenomenally successful. When I tell people my company name, they laugh, but they never forget it. The next time I meet them, they may have forgotten my surname, but they immediately say, "You're the 'In Your Face!' guy!"

One time at a chamber of commerce meeting I introduced myself with my company name, and three people

approached me to do business while two of my competitors were sitting in the same meeting.

I just did some pens for a prominent attorney I had never met. He was referred to me by a business friend of his, whom I had met casually several months before. The attorney's friend told him to call the "In Your Face!" guy and even gave him my phone number. This is continuing proof that memory hooks work!

"I'm Marvin Jeffreys, owner and operator of IBM. Yes, that's the IBM, Images by Marvin Portrait Studio, located in Maynardville, Tennessee."

"Remember, at Images by Marvin, we preserve memories in a flash!"

Marvin L. Jeffreys
Images by Marvin
Maynardville, TN

In an effort to set myself apart from other photographers, I started telling people, "I'm the owner and operator of IBM. I know you're wondering, and yes, that's *the* IBM, Images by Marvin Portrait Studio, located in Maynardville, Tennessee." Laughter always followed, but I immediately had the attention of any woman in the group. In my business, more than 90 percent of portrait buying decisions are made by women, and it's always my goal to reach the decision maker. I further use this hook with my personalized license plate, IBM-FOTO.

My second memory hook, "At Images by Marvin, we preserve memories in a flash!" came as a result of being challenged by my local BNI chapter to have a strong memory hook with which to close my one-minute infomercial. I accent this hook with a small portable strobe unit fired from behind me. Any new person who has been dozing immediately comes to full attention. If she didn't pay attention, believe me, she will the next time.

"When you need a phone, think Executone."

Dick Rieke
Executone
Teleconnect sales
Las Vegas, NV

I have been in sales management for twenty years and I always try to key in on "need" and "think" as important words to fit into any statement to clients. Since I'm in the phone business, the "hook" came pretty naturally. I use it in all my correspondence to clients. It seems to work; I've had some comments from them. One client told me he had received my letter several months earlier, and when he started having trouble with his phones, my hook jumped into his head and he called me first. By the way, I got the order.

The following are more examples of how to incorporate your business name into your memory hook.

"Starr Imprints: Advertise with a rising Starr."

Jane M. White
Starr Imprints
Specialty advertising
Rogersville, TN

"TRUST me."

Bob Carroll
Trust Funds
Hemet, CA

"Jafra, because together we're beautiful."

Jan Scott
Jafra Skin Care & Cosmetics
Newport Beach, CA

"Service is our middle name."

Scott Pedrick
Jasper's Service Pro
Carpet and upholstery cleaners
Sun Devil, AZ

"Let us help you show your true colors."

Kevin L. Pasternack
Truecolor Screen Print & Graphics
Tri-Town, Vernon, CT

"Placing investors FIRST."

Philip Heyl
First Investors
East Valley, AZ

Chapter
7

Communicate
Your Profession

Reminding Them of
What You Can Do for Them

MANY BUSINESSPEOPLE PLACE A LOT OF IMPORTANCE on telling the prospect what service or product they provide. This makes sense. However, other than the name of your business and perhaps an unusually informative logo or symbol, you have only your memory hook to let potential customers know why they may need what you sell.

The necessity of creating a professionally informative memory hook does not, however, stop the creative individual from using all the tricks available to make the hook memorable.

> *"I'm proud to be a provider of chiropractic services to the Mighty Ducks of Anaheim; that makes me the Official Quack for the group."*

Dr. Ken Cragen
Chiropractor
First Chiropractic of L.A.
Los Angeles, CA

Ten years of my own pride for my profession have historically been torn down by three little words coming from the mouths of friends, neighbors, even an occasional relative: "You're a quack!" As a chiropractor, I have worked hard, studied hard, and helped a lot of people. Still, those three little words have power over me.

Recently I had the opportunity to establish a professional relationship with our local hockey team, the Mighty Ducks of Anaheim. Shortly after the relationship was established, I received an official "duck call" in the mail, and that's when it hit me. If I'm a quack, it's perfectly fitting that I should be the Official Quack for the Mighty Ducks.

Now I laugh when someone calls me a quack, and I tell them this story. I bear the title of "quack" with honor instead of insult. Thanks to some creative thought and my exposure to the ideas of memory hooks, my self-esteem has taken a significant boost.

Dr. Cragen's approach deals head-on with the attitude that some people still have about chiropractic care. Years ago, in martial arts, I learned how to take someone's energy and turn it back in their direction. In a way, that is exactly what Dr. Cragen does—but with humor. He takes a negative comment or concern and tosses it back, or at least deflects it, in a way that gets people's attention and lets him address their stereotype.

"Bean counters with a difference."

Kris Krauskopf
Eisenberg & Krauskopf, CPAs
Tuckahoe, NY

I have owned my own accounting firm for fourteen years. Accountants have a bad reputation as "number crunchers" or "bean counters," so when I use my memory hook, I hold up a jar of jelly beans and get a laugh from the crowd. My point is that I'm an accountant that you can talk to and that I have a sense of humor. This memory hook has helped my business by making it easy for people to remember what I do and showing them that I'm approachable.

Naturally, our holiday gift of choice is boxes of Jelly Bellies!

This is an interesting memory hook with the same martial-arts twist as Dr. Cragen's message. Kris takes the age-old expression about accountants being "bean counters" and puts a memorable reverse spin on it. She makes it particularly effective by using her visual aid—the jar of jelly beans—whenever she introduces herself at networking groups.

"J. J. Casey's Florals—Flowers so real you'll think they need water."

Brenda Berkery
J. J. Casey's Florals
Rancho Santa Margarita, CA

I have a large basket filled with my artificial flowers that I leave on our boat dock step during the summer. During our first weeklong cruise one summer, I left the flowers on the dock. A neighbor on a live-aboard boat noticed them and, thinking I had neglected them for several days, came down armed with her watering can. When we returned from the trip, she rushed down to tell me how silly she felt when she discovered they were artificial!

On many occasions in my shop, people will ask me, "Are you sure those aren't real?" Artificial flowers have come a long way in the last few years, with a great deal of effort going into making them look like the real thing—even roses with artificial thorns!

Memory hooks such as J. J.'s are very effective. They are particularly useful when the person using them has the time to tell the story that Brenda shared with me. When there's a competitor on nearly every corner, as is often the case with florists, it is crucial that you stand out. Anyone who hears Brenda's memory hook and the story that goes with it will always think of her, even before they remember a florist who may be closer.

"I make you look good on paper!"

Diane Barretti
Printing Unlimited
Los Angeles, CA

I consider Printing Unlimited a custom printer—not just the print shop on every block you walk into when you want it back in an hour. So I started to tell everyone that "I can make you look good on paper." I repeated this at a chamber of commerce breakfast one day, and the publisher of our local newspaper stood up and remarked that out of everyone in the room he remembered what I did! It kind of stuck, and I started using it at BNI. I also use it on the calendar I put out each year and a flier I send as a thank-you.

Diane not only uses a memory hook in her presentations, she includes it in her marketing materials. This helps reinforce its effect. People such as the publisher of the local newspaper (it's always good to have the local newspaper publisher remember you among a large group of successful business profession-als) hear the message and then have it suc-cessfully reinforced by receiving addi-tional materials with the same message.

18	19	20 ●
25	26	27 ☾
Printing Unlimited will make you "LOOK GOOD ON PAPER"		

"It is in my interest to save you interest."

Pat McCormick
Norwest Mortgage, Inc.
Indianapolis, IN

With over eighteen years' experience in the mortgage banking field, I felt I must have a catchy, thought-provoking phrase to immediately get the public to listen to me—especially since I do a significant amount of selling by telephone. I joined the network over three years ago, but for a long time I resisted the idea of using a memory hook. That was a mistake. About fifteen months ago I was talking on the telephone and I mentioned to a client that it was "in my interest to save him interest." The phrase caught on.

When I conducted an open house for first-time buyers, I used the memory hook, and it caught their attention. I immediately had them listening to me. None of those attending had bought a home, but within three weeks I had three new customers, netting myself over $3,000. It works! Last year, I earned over $16,000 gross commission through my BNI networking alone.

"Imprisoned by paper? You need our files!"

Mollie Green
Sales representative
Creative Business Systems, Inc.
Knoxville, TN

By designing color-coded filing systems and space-saving filing cabinets, we at Creative Business Systems help people manage the huge amount of paperwork nearly all of us have to deal with. In every office there are times when employees feel overwhelmed by the amount of paperwork they have, or panicked when a vital file is misplaced. Then they do indeed feel "imprisoned" by paper. Our files are the way out!

"Helping you secure the financial future you want."

Joyce Theis
Financial planner
Financial Design Group
Portland, OR

Since I can work with almost any type of financial goal, I decided I needed a memory hook that could and would apply to anyone in every case. This hook is not necessarily cute or catchy, but it is very applicable to any person or business. I use it when asked, "What is it that you do?" When I answer, "I help you secure the financial future you want!" I generally get back a question like "What do you mean?" This allows me to say, "Well, it depends on what you want. I have a number of systems, methods, etc., to help you figure it out." The memory hook leads right into more questions and a more detailed discussion of the scope of my business.

"My life insurance is so good, it's to die for."

David Machry
London Life Insurance Company
Etobicoke, Ontario, Canada

Effective conversation is most important in my profession. My memory hook is an example of my sense of humor, which I use to maintain a positive atmosphere while getting my point across.

When people think about life insurance, they automatically think about death. Generally, death is the last thing people want to talk about—but it cannot be ignored if I'm to make proper recommendations regarding someone's financial security program. Therefore, my memory hook represents my business approach: to the point, but with feeling!

"Let someone who's been there tell you where to go!"

Leni Maier
Travel agent
ATC Travel, Inc.
N. Tarrytown, NY

My memory hook was actually given to me by one of my BNI fellow members, Gene Krachell. He, being a creative type, invented it for me and has helped me use it on a regular basis. It has been fun to use, and I have gotten good responses with it, but I must admit that I have trouble remembering it and have to refer to my notes occasionally.

"So, don't forget—When you have a question about tax, come to Millstone for the facts."

Joyce Guerrera, CPA
Millstone Accounting Services, P.C.
Pigeon Forge, TN

Well, it took me a very, very long time to find the right memory hook. Everybody else in my networking group had memory hooks—some cute, some funny, some trying various ones out for response by the group. I had nothing. What rhymes with "accounting"? My husband, who's very creative, said, "Well, you do more than just accounting, you do taxes as well." This got me thinking, and being an avid crossword puzzler, I started trying to rhyme "tax"— ax, bax, cax—and I eventually got to "fax." Ahh, this one will work, I thought, if I change the spelling to "facts." And so a memory hook was born.

"Ninety percent of all accidents happen in the home. So travel!"

"If you can afford to travel first class, and don't, your heirs will!"

Lance Mead
Lunar Travel Agency Ltd.
Yonkers, NY

The best results I've ever gotten when using my memory hook was at a chamber mixer. When I told my name and company and ended with the memory hook, everyone applauded. Even more important, at the end of the mixer the coordinator went out of his way to ask if anyone remembered the travel agent. Needless to say, everyone did. In fifteen or twenty seconds, I had left a lasting impression on the crowd.

Regarding "If you don't travel first class, your heirs will," I believe it has allowed me to sell up! The truth is that more members have now asked "How much is business or first class?" I also believe that it places a question in members' minds concerning possibly something better. As for my other memory hook, I believe the fact that it's done with humor has been well received by members and guests. They know I'm creative and fun!

"I make taxes less taxing."

Robert L. Kailes, CPA
Tax accountant
Playa del Rey, CA

We take a two-step approach to our memory hook. First, we make taxes less taxing by helping our clients prepare their tax returns in the least "taxing" (i.e., painful) way possible. We individualize ways for our clients to gather their tax information as comfortably and yet as completely as possible, thereby making the preparation less taxing. Secondly, we make taxes less taxing to our clients by legally reducing their taxes. Through our experience, knowledge, and continued education, we feel that our clients pay lower taxes.

"Is the snapshot of your financial choices the masterpiece it should be?"

Martha E. Laff, CLU
Financial consultant
Financial Focus
Santa Clarita, CA

I have been writing articles and offering monthly discussion programs in my office, titled "Financial Focus." When my clients focus their financial choices, they are attempting to improve or adjust the vision they have in this part of their life. When the picture is focused and at its best, they treasure what it signifies, work to preserve it, and hopefully the plan becomes a "masterpiece" for now and the future. It takes my clients' willingness to identify goals, listen, and take action, along with my experience and guidance, to create financial masterpieces that protect them now and leave a lasting legacy of financial freedom and balance.

$\big\uparrow_{\jmath}$

"My pictures say a thousand words, so you don't have to."

Robert Stewart
Robert Stewart Photography, Ltd.
Royal Oak, MI

Everyone has heard the saying "A picture is worth a thousand words." I took this phrase and applied it to my business, corporate photographic illustrations. Almost every picture I take is trying to sell something. If I am successful and take a good picture, I implant desire, curiosity, and craving in the prospect's head. When the prospect goes to my client wanting more information, the client gets a prospect who is already warmed up, so my client doesn't have to say as much. Ergo, I have just saved him a thousand words.

During my 60-second presentations at weekly networking meetings, I usually talk about the importance of a good picture to sell the product or service, then close with my hook, which usually brings a smile.

$\big\uparrow_{\jmath}$

"I can't put Humpty-Dumpty back together again, but I can sue the person who pushed him off the wall!"

Thomas W. Teixeira
Personal injury attorney
O'Brien, Shafner, Stuart, Kelly & Morris, P.C.
Groton, CT

I developed my memory hook after settling a very significant case for a middle-aged man who had suffered a traumatic brain injury in an automobile accident. While I certainly felt euphoric that I played a role in getting this kind man

71

enough money to ensure that he could live comfortably for the rest of his life, I was profoundly saddened that I could do nothing to put this man back together again—to give him back the life he had before the accident.

I found a way to express my feelings in a memory hook that has three distinct advantages. First, it explains exactly what kind of legal work I perform. Second, it sends a message that I am approachable, that I am not a stuffed shirt but have a sense of humor about my work. There's nothing like a smile to break the ice when meeting someone for the first time. Third, it is a memory hook that reminds me of my limited role in the lives of injured people. I can't make everything right, but I can make someone pay.

The way I found this memory hook is interesting. It came to me in a flash one night as I was taking a shower after having read my kids a bedtime story—Humpty-Dumpty!

"Let me take the world off your shoulders."

Sharon Howard
Massage therapist
Cleveland, TN

I came up with my memory hook because of my love for clichés, puns, and words. Most people who come to me for massage have incredible amounts of stress and tension stored in their neck and shoulders. So—I combined the saying "weight of the world on my shoulders" with my ability to relieve the stress and tension, and I got "Let me take the world off your shoulders." Customers often moan or sigh when I repeat it.

Here are more profession-specific memory hooks that people have presented to me and to fellow BNI members.

"I believe in the tooth, the whole tooth, and nothing but the tooth, so help me God."

Dr. Joe Wilson
Dentist
Glendale, CA

"A business without a sign is a sign of no business."

Ray DeLeone
Sign company
Canyon Springs, CA

"Only your travel agent can tell you where to go."

Pat Yee
Travel agent
Honolulu, HI

"We provide life after death."

Jack Knight
Insurance
Yucaipa, CA

"We put your best face forward."

Mary Whitman
Cosmetics
Redlands, CA

"Dust is my business."

Diane Licciardi
Mary Maids
Redlands, CA

"I have the owner's manual for your mind."

Linda Garcia
Hypnotherapist
Los Feliz, CA

"I love the heat."

Jim Lakner
Heating and air conditioning
Hemet, CA

"I am your own personal disaster preparedness contact."

Anne Wertz
Life insurance
Los Feliz, CA

"I can help your business look better on paper than it really is."

Dorothy Winkel
Desktop publishing
Canyon Springs, CA

"If you wear out your body, where are you going to live?"

Dr. Catherine Devore
Chiropractor
Suns, AZ

"Your pain is our pleasure!"

Victoria Outmans
Oral surgeon
Huntington Beach, CA

"We measure success one investor at a time!"

Tom Hanson
Stockbroker
Huntington Beach, CA

"I sell the houses you put your home into!"

Kathy Paugh
Real estate
Westminster, CA

"Our firm is hard on numbers and soft on people!"

Mark Guillod
Certified Public Accountant
Costa Mesa, CA

> **"I take care of your computer so you can take care of your business."**

Robert McNutt
Computer consultant
Glenwood Springs, CO

> **"Computel—we'll help you communicate with confidence."**

Deena Regier
Business telephone systems and facsimile
Long Beach, CA

> **"If you have teeth or want teeth, give us a call!"**

Pat Lester
Dental services
Tustin, CA

> **"Travel is my trip."**

Rosemary Hall
Travel consultant
Newport Beach, CA

> **"We don't let dirt get past us."**

Barbara Kinkade
Ace Cleaning Services
Salt Lake City, UT

"I don't have good hands, I'm just your good neighbor."

Frank Jones
State Farm Insurance
Fountain Valley, CA

"Be a guest at your own party."

Carol Zapadka
Full-service catering
Tri-Town, Vernon, CT

"Silence at a discount."

Ian Melmed
Meineke Mufflers
Tri-Town, Vernon, CT

"Beauty in a box."

Rennie Kesterson
Cosmetics and skin care
Las Vegas, NV

"We discuss your occasion for a few minutes so you can be remembered forever."

Diane Verdaasdonk
D&D Gift Baskets
Lancaster, CA

"If you know somebody who wants to move, tell them to call me and start packing!"

> Barbara Karvelas
> Real estate agent
> Huntington Beach, CA

"The original party animal."

> R. David Hackenbruch
> Bartender
> Indianapolis, IN

"The buck starts with Edward D. Jones & Co."

> Edward D. Jones
> Investment representative
> Indianapolis, IN

"Call Atlantic North American for a moving experience!"

> Wayne LaMade
> National accounts representative
> Indianapolis, IN

"If you don't know the difference between software and silverware, give me a call."

Sally Dicken
Computer consultant
Monrovia, CA

"Carving memories one stone at a time."

Stanley Pulver Jr.
Memorials
Mid Westchester, NY

"We make the business side of your business less taxing."

Russ Whitehouse
Certified Public Accountant
Salt Lake City, UT

"Our business takes the stress out of yours."

Edward J. Waters
Stress reduction services
Phoenix, AZ

"I sell peace of mind, not a piece of the rock!"

Al Sutton
Insurance
Ottawa, OH

"We make your money work as hard as you do."

Bob Cullen
Financial planner
Covina, CA

"Round trip airfare—14 cents (per minute)!"

Jackie Maugh
Long-distance service
Las Vegas, NV

"If it computes, we sell it. If it doesn't, we repair it."

Patrick LaBash
Computer sales and service
Saguaro, AZ

"Our unlucky clients come to us by accident; the rest are referred."

Raymond Arenofsky
Accident lawyer
Foothills, AZ

"It's better to advertise your products, than your business, for sale."

Oscar Bovolini
Printing and graphics
Huntington Beach, CA

"Home is where the heart is; I'd like to find your heart a new home."

Barbara Grimes
Real estate agent
Fountain Valley, CA

"If you are ill-legal, come to the Juris doctor."

Brian Daily
Lawyer
Birmingham, MI

"The IRS tells you right off, it's written in CODE. You need me, I'm the DE-CODER."

Lucygne O'ffill
Accountant
Orange, CA

"I fix $8 haircuts!"

Christine Stock
Hair stylist
Diamond Bar, CA

"I'll help you create a first impression that's worth a second look."

Richard Scoby
Graphic design
Fountain Valley, CA

"The name of my game is C.Y.A.—Cover Your Assets."

Scott Pierson
Tax preparation
Rancho Santa Margarita, CA

"There are two words in show business. I take care of both."

Doug Taylor
Musician
Las Vegas, NV

"Insider trading is legal if you're a networker!"

J. R. Chick Gallagher
Executive Director, BNI
Delaware and Southeast Pennsylvania

"Yes, Virginia, creating referrals for your business is our business at BNI!"

K. Lynn Morgan
Executive Director, BNI
Virginia

"BNI is the IBM of word-of-mouth marketing."

Don Morgan
Executive Director, BNI
Canada

"Cold calls and cold cereal vs. hot referrals and a hot breakfast? No contest."

Candace Bailly
Executive Director, BNI
Central South Oregon

"I'm the Dr. of dollars."

John Miller
Financial planner
Rancho Santa Margarita, CA

"We bring color to your life!"

Andrea Kramer
Florist
Yucaipa, CA

Chapter

8

Tell Them Quality Is Important to You

Showing Them You're Serious about Your Work

MANY BUSINESSPEOPLE TAKE PRIDE in being more than just competent, in doing a highly professional job, whatever their specialty. And many customers look for the vendor who can communicate that sense of pride in a job well done. Most buyers would rather pay a little extra, perhaps even a lot, to get a product that will perform well and last or to get a service job done right the first time.

In word-of-mouth marketing, of course, networking is the way to spread the reputation of being good at what you do. But you can also jump start your word-of-mouth marketing by communicating up front that you're serious about your work.

The following memory hooks demonstrate an emphasis on quality. Although they use other common hook techniques, such as word play, the primary message of these people and businesses is, in effect, "We want you to consider us above our competitors simply because we take pains to satisfy the customer."

"I do a twelve-point checkup of your current brochure needs."

Dave Voracek
Marketing and advertising consultant
The Brochure Doctor
Arlington, VA

This is a visual memory hook. When he presents himself to a group, Dave stands out from the other "men in suits": he wears a doctor's white lab coat.

I've been in business since 1982 as a marketing consultant, generally providing advertising-agency services to small and medium-sized companies. The trouble is, when you tell people you're a marketing consultant, it generally doesn't register; it goes in one ear and out the other. I would go to chamber of commerce functions and other events, and all the men were in suits and nobody made a lasting impression. I was just another guy in a blue suit.

About the same time, I started doing seminars about how small businesses could create effective brochures and direct-mail pieces. I realized that most business people did not feel officially "in business" until they had some kind of brochure to hand out. The most basic marketing tool they wanted and needed was a brochure. Hence, "marketing" equals "brochure."

Creating a persona to present the memory hook is one of the most creative tricks I've seen. There's only one drawback to this approach: Dave tells me that the Brochure Doctor impression sometimes works too well. People sometimes get the impression that he creates only brochures; they don't think of him for other marketing needs. So he tries to work into the conversation that his firm also does direct mail, newsletters, fliers, and other printed marketing tools. He also says that people have a tendency to forget his real name. People who haven't seen him for a while often introduce him to others without using his name because they don't remember it. But they do remember his hook, and they introduce him as "the Brochure Doctor."

When you're marketing advertising services, you are really selling other businesses on your creativity. Marketing is all about standing out from the crowd. When you make a memorable and positive impression on people you meet in a crowded room, you're demonstrating that you know how to make a long-standing business—in this case, your own—stand out with a fresh approach.

"Remarkable!"

Norm Dominguez
Executive Director, BNI Southwest
Arizona and New Mexico

When someone asks you, "How are you?" the standard response is "fine," "okay," "all right," or some such. This kind of response is often an untruth; in reality, things may be on the great side or may need a bit of help. Thus, instead

of an untruth, I decided to give a simple response—
"Remarkable!" At first, I got looks of bewilderment. But
after months of planting the "Remarkable" seed, I had
created an expectation. Now it has become a life style, a
belief that life is remarkable, a way of generating energy.

This memory hook is my way of establishing a communica-
tive link with anyone, any time—a lasting impression in the
word-of-mouth world!

"Rolls Royce service at a low cost!"

Joy Jones
Joy Jones Insurance Agency
Stafford, TX

I am an insurance agent in the greater Houston area, where
there are hundreds of agents. Since we are a woman-owned
business in a service industry, we wanted to set ourselves
apart from the run-of-the-mill agents.

The story behind our memory hook is this: There was once
a very wealthy and famous man in Houston named Jim

ROLLS ROYCE SERVICE AT A LOW COST!

Brady. His nickname was "Diamond Jim." We started looking in the antique stores and finally found an old picture of his home. We reproduced this picture in postcards and used them in direct mail advertising. It's been very successful.

"Your professional between the sheets!"

Donald E. Hart
Hart Printers, Inc.
Lancaster, CA

When I rose to give my presentation, I had to speak up to make myself heard; there was a lot of conversation going on. After I presented this memory hook, however, the crowd listened attentively.

I know the importance of memory hooks; our BNI chapter has made it a point to encourage every member to have one. One of the stimulus games we use is to have everyone present his memory hook over three weeks of meetings, then hold a contest in which every member writes down all the other memory hooks he can remember. We award a prize to anyone who can remember them all.

My memory hook has been successful, even though I haven't noticed many customers repeating it.

"Your success is our business."

John R. Meyer
Executive Director, BNI
Toledo, Ohio

As much as we preach to our members the importance of having a memory hook, we realized that we did not have one ourselves. We believe wholeheartedly that everyone should have a hook, and we are no exception.

When we first adopted this memory hook, I was at a chapter meeting. I was the fifth or sixth person to give my 60-second commercial and the first to use a memory hook. When I was done, every person after me used his or her memory hook. As the president started the next part of the meeting, he was interrupted by the first six people; they explained that they had forgotten to use their memory hooks and wanted to let everyone know what they were. People who use them benefit from them; people who don't, wish they had.

We've gotten a very positive reaction to ours. It reminds members why we're there and reassures them that we want to help them succeed. Nonmembers hear our memory hook and want more information on how we can help them be successful.

The following memory hooks are also aimed primarily at communicating a generic message of quality.

"If you think a professional is expensive, wait until you hire an amateur."

Howard Greenspon
Video inventory services
Las Vegas, NV

"Quality shows in every move we make."

Russ Roman
United Van Lines
Foothills, AZ

"The fussier-than-you-are printer."

> Bruce Davis
> Printing and graphics
> Portland, ME

"We don't cut corners—we clean them!"

> Jeanne Ainsley
> Cleaning service
> Albuquerque, NM

"We don't cut corners—we build them."

> David Koller
> Builder
> Bowling Green, OH

"If we don't sweep you off your feet, we're not satisfied!"

> Debbie Haun
> Janitorial services
> Temecula, CA

"If quality is a major factor, call your licensed contractor."

> Bob Baker
> Remodeling
> Santa Ana, CA

"A cut above the rest."

John Laney
Lawn care
Sylvania, OH

"Lights! Camera! Action!
We guarantee satisfaction!"

Craig & Linda Campana
Videographers
Image Associates, Ltd.
Milwaukee, WI

"Intelligent people know facts.
Successful people know people."

Susan Butler
Executive Director, BNI
Washington, DC

"It's not WHAT you know or WHO you know, it's HOW
WELL you know them that makes a difference."

Elisabeth Misner
Director of Public Relations
BNI

C h a p t e r

9

Educate As You Sell

Telling Them What Your Business Does

ONE OF THE MAJOR FUNCTIONS OF ADVERTISING, of course, is to give the prospect information about your product or service. Sometimes this involves simply telling the potential customer why your product or service is preferable to your competitor's. At other times, however, you need to persuade the prospect that your product or service is something she needs. Your message may be in the nature of a reminder, or it may be an education from the ground up about something the prospect has never considered or even heard of.

"I help you build a sound mind and a sound body so your business can achieve sound profits."

Jeffry C. Hoy
One 2 One Personal Training
Cleveland, TN

As a professional personal trainer, my main goal is to teach clients how to achieve a higher quality of living through nutrition and fitness techniques. These techniques are major factors in building a sound mind and a sound body, which can help you achieve sound profits.

Building a sound body means increasing lean muscle mass and decreasing body fat. This leads ultimately to an increase in the body's metabolism, allowing the body to burn energy (calories) at a significantly higher rate. The sum of these effects helps develop a sound mind, because looking and feeling healthy provides the confidence to perform professional duties at higher levels of effectiveness and efficiency. On the business bottom line, this translates to sound profits.

"We look beyond the numbers."

"We do numbers so you don't have to."

C. Trevor McMurray
Forensic accountant
Carter, Young, Lankford, & Roach, P.C.
Bristol, TN

A regular auditor deals only with numbers. As forensic accountants, we have to look beyond the numbers and look at the nature of the transactions to guard against fraud. I came up with this quote after hearing the AICPA's "No one looks beyond the numbers like a CPA." I thought my quote fit our forensic accounting division.

I came up with the second memory hook while listening to Dan Rawls, our local BNI director, speak at a chapter meeting. He was talking about how we need to listen to everything people say so we can analyze their needs. I feel that most people are afraid of numbers and taxes. That is where we come in. We do the numbers so you don't have to.

"Columbus discovered America—but it was a woman who financed his trip."

Diane Haneklau
Certified Financial Planner
St. Louis, MO

This memory hook is a revision of something I heard in a seminar for women. How do people react? They're amused.

> **"Networking is like banking—you have to make deposits before you can take withdrawals."**

Alice Ostrower
Executive Director, BNI
Connecticut

We live in a society that has a drive-in window expectancy with credit-card purchasing. These concepts are contradictory to quality networking. There is no instant reward, and you can't develop long-term relationships on credit!

You can't buy good networking. It is an investment in the most valuable and irreplaceable commodity we all share: our time. The time you spent is gone; it can never be replaced. No amount of money can buy it back. Money can be accumulated and lost, then regained—but not time. So who you spend your time with and how you spend your time are crucial.

Networking is like banking—for good cash flow, be sure you have more deposits than withdrawals.

> **"We make something out of nothing."**

Coleman Moore
Consulting engineer
Raleigh, NC

When familiar memory hooks are used on a regular basis, I've seen chapter members eagerly await a memory hook from a member. If the member forgets to give the memory hook, the other members shout it out in unison. I've seen this happen with my memory hook (I design computerized industrial and manufacturing equipment) and several others.

Several chapter members have prompted me on my memory hook when I have overlooked it.

A businessman in a local chapter created a wonderful memory hook. He would always stand up and say, "I'm in the go-away business. I just want you to go away!" Guests would always look perplexed until he added, "I'm your travel agent! I want everyone to go away!"

I attended one meeting in which, although the chapter was only a few months old, the members were already familiar with each other. During the 60-second commercial portion of the meeting, the attorney slowly stood up. With a bowed head, he said, "My business is closing. . . ." Silence engulfed the room. I was shocked. Everyone looked around. Members who hadn't been paying attention stopped to stare at him. After a few seconds he excitedly said, "I'm a real estate attorney. I specialize in real estate closings!" He received such a response from the group that this became his weekly memory hook.

> **"I am your Money Finder. I teach people to find money for YOU just because they want to!"**

Andra Brack
Executive Director, BNI
Indianapolis, IN

I have been using this for about nine months. The immediate response every time I use it, whether at a BNI meeting or anywhere else, is always a chuckle or two. (Then I know I have their attention!) The majority of the time, someone responds with, "Wow, I like that! Can you find money for me?" or some other response indicating that they want to hear what I have to say.

I have also observed over the last month or two that those who have heard my memory hook before are beginning to introduce me as "Andra Brack, the Money Finder—she really can get people to find you money!"

> **"How old you ARE is your business. How old you LOOK is mine."**

Stephanie Lara
Mary Kay Cosmetics
Northridge, CA

This is actually a quote from the great lady herself, Mary Kay. When I read it recently in her book, I felt it was perfect to adapt as my own memory hook because, when it comes to teaching good skin care, it's so easy to identify with. The phrase is appropriate for both men and women, and the products in the basic Mary Kay skin care line are formulated to reduce the appearance of aging and improve our looks. Chapter members and visitors have repeated the phrase to others because it's fun, it's to the point, and it's easy to remember.

Here are some other educational memory hooks:

> **"Beware of what you're thinking—someone is listening."**

Marty Renger
Self-talk trainer
Irvine, CA

"You don't have to feel bad to feel better."

Gary Brownlee
Bodyworks
South Bay, CA

"Would you rather pay taxes on your interest, or earn interest on your taxes?"

Lee Ann Zerbel
State Farm Insurance
Bel Air, CA

"You don't have to floss all your teeth—just the ones you want to keep!"

Dr. Alan Miller
Dentist
Costa Mesa, CA

"A pop beats a pill for pain."

Dr. John A. Vogel
Chiropractor
Lancaster, CA

"Using Host Dry Cleaning, you don't have to walk on water to have clean carpet."

Ardiss McDonald and Marlin Fisher
Cleaning services
Santa Maria, CA

"Tax avoidance is legal; tax evasion is not!"

Linda Brown
Accountant, tax preparer
Rochester, MI

"If you don't know the difference between a CD that plays and a CD that pays, you need to call me."

James R. Larew
Financial consultant
Monrovia, CA

"If you don't want to retire, that's your business. If you _do_ want to retire, that's our business."

Catherine Herod
Investment advisor
A. G. Edwards & Sons, Inc.
Knoxville, TN

Chapter

10

Rhyme It
or Sing It

Making Them Hum
Your Ad for Hours

S OME RHYME SHORT; some rhyme long;
      Some rhyme lyrically, much like a song.
Some rhyme well; others rhyme wrong;
      We like 'em anyway—just play along.

(Performed like a Gilbert & Sullivan patter song:)

You're lying awake in your four-poster bed
  With nightmares of brochures and ads in your head.
They keep flying around and will give you no peace
  'cause each has a deadline in under two weeks.
Oh! What can you do? You've known the deadline for months!
  You thought you would do it on time—just this once.
You're tossing and turning instead of sound sleeping
  And into your head an idea comes creeping.
There in the mire of covers and sweat
  You remember there's help, there's hope for you yet.
You know whom to call; you've seen her at meetings;
  You'll pick up a phone and give her a greeting.
It's Jacque of Foreman Graphics with ideas aplenty
  At eight one eight/seven nine four/ninety-six twenty.

Jacque Foreman
Graphic designer & typesetter
Foreman Graphics
Altadena, CA

Some years ago I became a member of the Women's Referral Service. They have what is called a Round Robin, in which each member stands and delivers a one-minute presentation. They meet monthly. After about six months, I just plain got tired of sounding as dull and un-thought-out as everyone else. Nobody stood out in my memory, and I wanted to stand out in the memory of others.

One day, while listening to the radio, I heard a commercial that was set to one of Gilbert & Sullivan's patter songs. I decided that I could do that too.

So I did. And my first rhyming commercial was born. What I found out was that I was no more nervous delivering a rehearsed presentation than I was lamely thinking on my feet—in fact, maybe a little less. Not only that, but I had a real feeling of accomplishment when I was finished. The applause didn't hurt my ego either!

After that I realized that not only would I get bored if I did the same rhyme every time, but so would everyone else. So I decided to make one for each of the different facets of what I do. Brochures and ads are two of the items that I create for clients, and I usually get the job after they have spent weeks (maybe months) trying to do it themselves. So I decided to make fun of the fact that I usually get short deadlines. Thus came the one that goes, "You're lying awake in your four-poster bed. . . ."

Has this penchant for rhyme brought me business? Let's put it this way: no one forgets who it is that does the graphic design, typesetting, and pen and ink drawings. And members have received phone calls asking for the phone number of that funny person who does the rhymes.

I envy the creativity of the person who can write (then sing) like Jacque. It takes a talented person. However, what I've found is that there are many talented people in the business world who just don't take the chance to highlight their abilities. When someone puts this kind of effort into a brief presentation, people listen. When you're in business, that's exactly what you need—for people to listen and hear your message. In a networking environment, you're competing with many other people. Using a technique like this definitely lets you to stand out in the crowd.

> **"When you think about your future and your head hangs low,**
>
> **Don't fret, just call Joe!"**

Joe Hansen
Insurance
Primerica Financial Services
Burbank, CA

I find after being in financial services over eight years that people are worried about the future. Due to busy lives and a lack of education, people just don't plan. I do this hook in front of the group right after I talk about the stock market, and everyone gets excited and laughs. I have gotten a ton of business using memory hooks in this network; it's awesome! I think a memory hook is very important so everyone will remember you and know you're different.

The primary use of a memory hook is to get business. Even simple memory hooks such as this one can accomplish that goal. The reason for this is, as Joe says, that "everyone will remember you and know you're different."

> **"If your networking's not working and your leads are low,**
>
> **Call me, Penny Palmer, and I'll help your business grow!"**

Penny Palmer
Regional Director, BNI
Orange County/South Bay, CA

As I visit my BNI chapters, I give workshops that will help members network effectively. At the Orange, California, chapter, we did a memory-hook workshop and broke up into groups of three to bounce ideas off each other. Dave Weiss and Dr. Chris Gaukler gave me some good ideas, and it was Dave's spontaneous creativity that set my memory hook into the rhyme I use.

"Travel stress free,
with no service fee;

Remember Sharrie Long,
and you'll never go wrong."

Sharrie Long
Madre Hills Travel
Sierra Madre, CA

Listening to different people give their memory hooks made me think about mine. I realized that a lot of travel agencies are now charging a service fee. Also, most travel agents don't take the time to research for the best fare and check on the reservations periodically to ensure that their clients travel stress-free. Whenever possible, I request seats for my clients in advance. I also issue boarding passes to save them time at the airport. I put all these factors together and came up with my memory hook.

I've had the memory hook made into a stamp, and now I'm stamping the backs of my business cards. I hope this will help my clients remember me whenever they need to travel.

I can personally attest to the accuracy of Sharrie's memory hook. She's been my travel agent for over four years!

"You are not alone, when you need a loan."

Jim Nassar
Mortgage banker
Colony Mortgage Corporation
Holland, OH

One of the most common problems lenders face is that our clients are sometimes reluctant to disclose financial or credit information to us. When this happens, it's difficult to know what's best for the client. It's like a doctor trying to diagnose a patient and knowing only half of the symptoms.

To avoid this situation, I try to make the clients understand that I am on their side. Once my clients realize this, they open up and tell me everything that's pertinent. Thus, my memory hook stresses the fact that I'm there to help them—in other words, they are not alone. They have me on their side.

(Sung to the tune of "Jingle Bells":)

"Dashing to Doc Snow's
Smiling all the way

He'll straighten out your teeth
And relieve your TMJ.

When our telephone rings
We pick it up real quick

And get you in for a free exam
In time for Ol' St. Nick!"

106

> "Your pearly whites should be straight and bright;
> Call Snow Orthodontics before tonight."

Renee Mullins
Gilbert H. Snow, DDS
Orthodontics
Palmdale, CA

In his book *The World's Best Known Marketing Secret,* Dr. Misner encourages all his readers to write down their memory hooks. I'm the kind of person who just loves cute and catchy phrases. I'm usually operating at a hundred miles an hour, and I've found that a memorable hook lets me introduce a fellow networker's business to someone new very easily, and a really good hook just comes to mind so quickly.

Brace Yourself

Gilbert H. Snow, D.D.S. - High Ropes Challenge

and smile!

Dr. Snow is accepting new patients.
Call today for your complimentary orthodontic consultation.

1-800-Dr-Snows

151 East Avenue J
Lancaster
(805) 945-2771

GILBERT H. SNOW
D.D.S. INC.
Healthy smiles for adults and children

247 E. Palmdale Blvd.
Palmdale
(805) 273-1750

So, anyway, I'm sitting at this breakfast thinking that I'm tired of my old line, "Let us set you straight," and I noticed a lady across the room with a very pretty pearl necklace (they must have been really big pearls!) Pearls, pearly whites—that got my pencil racing across the back of one of the fliers at my table, and I came up with not one but several new hooks: "Just say Snow!" "Brace yourself—smile by Snow Orthodontics!" and "Smile—someone will notice."

"Why squint when you can tint?"

Mary Rousseve
Sol Cal Window Tinting
Diamond Bar, CA

I knew I wanted something that rhymes when putting together a memory hook, because rhymes are easiest to remember. It just happened to be at a time when my father-in-law, Tom Rousseve, was in town visiting. I asked him to help me think of one. He is very familiar with our business and knows that one benefit of window tinting, besides heat reduction, is glare reduction. So of course when he came up with "Why squint when you can tint?" it seemed perfect because it was so easy to remember!

I use my memory hook at my networking meetings and will incorporate it into some of our advertising this year.

"Take your wreck to AutoTek."

Lisa Boushey
AutoTek
Collision repair
St. Peters, MO

Sitting at a Dairy Queen one day during the construction of our facility, we brainstormed the phrase "Take your wreck to AutoTek." It's featured on the first paperwork customers see, so they are subliminally programmed.

We're soon putting up a billboard that says, "Don't get lost in the MAZE of confusion; take your wreck to AutoTek!" (MAZE is a competitor across the highway.)

> *"First the loan, then the home;*
> *Loans that don't groan*
> *And homes that don't roam."*

Steve Marche
Mortgage broker
Great American Funding Corporation
Westlake Village, CA

One variation of my memory hook tells how we do great home loans, but not mobile-home loans. Memory hooks have really worked for me. A woman in my network group called us up, and the first words out of her mouth were, "I know, first the loan, then the home." We both had a good laugh. Then she proceeded to tell me that she had remembered our LCD [Lowest Common Denominator] when she set out to look for a new home. A young man who recently called me told me that I had spoken to him six months earlier and that he remembered, "First the loan, then the home; not the car, as it may roam." He remembered not to buy or lease the car, as it would affect his ability to purchase a new home. He saved his money, and all through the six months he remembered our LCD.

As my son and I drove down Thousand Oaks Boulevard in Westlake Village, all of a sudden we heard a horn honking and a person screaming. My son asked, "What's that, Daddy?" It was one of our clients, one we had served well, screaming at me: "I know! First the loan, then the home, not the car!" as he drove his new BMW convertible close to my car. "Now I have my home and my new car, thanks to you!"

> **"From floor to ceiling, window to wall,
> Call Crystal Clean Connection, we do it all!"**

Flory Kemp Peterson and Sharyl McGowan
Crystal Clean Connection
Housekeeping, window and carpet cleaning
Azusa, CA

We started by asking for ideas that incorporated all the services we provided in our housekeeping business. Someone mentioned "From floor to ceiling, window to wall," and that sounded like a good foundation that included everything we offered in our business. When we presented it at the network breakfast meeting, it stuck. Simple story, but true.

> **"The creative guy with the creative tie."**

Dennis R. Green
Dennis Green Advertising
Farmington Hills, MI

I love to wear bold, unusual ties. I have a large collection—probably close to a hundred—of Nicole Miller, Jerry Garcia, Disney, Warner Brothers, and other wild ties. They come in a wide variety of colors and patterns. One of my fellow members, a woman, imitated me once by wearing a wild tie to a meeting and doing her presentation as if she were me!

My memory hook evolved because I wear the ties and because I'm in the creativity business. I own an advertising agency and do most of the creative writing myself.

I've started using my hook on the Internet. I've advertised on America Online with a bulk e-mail service. I recently established an Internet home page—http://www.adcomm.com/green/—where I also use my memory hook.

"If you're wasting money throwing food away,
Don't get upset, don't pull your hair,
Just call Vicki for Tupperware."

Vicki Bart
Tupperware sales representative
Covina, CA

The reason I came up with my memory hook is because I keep hearing from customers how they have to throw away the food in their cupboards and their refrigerators.

Sometimes they have to throw away all their boxes of cereal, rice, and wheat products because of moths and weevils. When their food is in Tupperware, that problem doesn't happen. So I also tell customers, "If your cupboards are bugging you, you need to see me."

Sometimes I hear how the food in their refrigerator keeps growing mold. So I let my customers know that although Tupperware won't preserve food forever, it does help food last two to three times longer.

"If your hair is fried and dyed and laid to the side,
Call Janet so you won't have to hide."

Janet Rios
Maxim Hair Salon
Downey, CA

My memory hook was created when a walk-in client came into the salon with bleached blond hair that looked like steel wool. It was a spur-of-the-moment remark! We got together at my first job and I made up this memory hook.

111

That's not all the song and rhyme by a long shot. Here are some more, mostly short and punchy, memory hooks that come on like one-liners in a Broadway musical.

"We protect your money and your honey."

Paul Ryan
Alarm company
Yucaipa, CA

"You'll feel fine when your spine's in line."

Dr. Diane Bellwood
Chiropractor
Covina, CA

"Your retirement
won't be too sunny

If you have too much month
at the end of your money."

Marjorie Stanford
Certified Financial Planner
Fountain Valley, CA

"Come on down, we'll do a crown."

Dr. Larry Brown
Dentist
Mission Valley, CA

"Before you turn to dust,
Come see me for your will or trust."

Sue Kraft
Attorney
Covina, CA

"I have the tools at my command
To keep more money in your hand."

Stephanie Roderick
Tax preparer
Los Feliz, CA

"For balloons with a flair,
Remember the bear in the air."

Steve Kromer
Bear Balloons
Laguna Hills, CA

"A roof done right is water-tight,
But a roof done wrong won't last too long!"

Ken McCarthy
Roofer
Anaheim, CA

"We have miles of smiles!"

Dr. Rosellen Kimbrough
Dentist
Yucaipa, CA

*"Jack and Jill climbed up the hill
   onto the corporate ladder.*

*Now Jack loved Jill and Jill loved Jack.
   So, what could be the matter?*

*All seemed well and life was swell
   'Til bill time came around.*

*Then Jack blamed Jill, Jill blamed Jack
   'cause time could not be found.*

*Their lack of time was out of sight,
   Their problems astronomical!*

*Their main concerns, as you can see
   weren't merely economical.*

*Now, Jack and Jill climb up the hill
   just to enjoy the view.*

*Pay-EZ . . . The best reason why not to pay the
   bills."*

Susan Parker
Pay-EZ
Bill-paying service
Paradise Valley, AZ

"When you're in a commotion,
Who're you gonna call? Law in motion!"

Gloria Jones
Paralegal
Long Beach, CA

"If your records are in a mess
Or the IRS is causing you stress,
Come, confess!"

Wendy Martin
Certified Public Accountant
Salt Lake City, UT

"We insure your business, auto, house.

We even insure your diamonds, Picasso and
spouse.

We also handle life, disability and health.

We want to insure all your wealth."

Marsha Aizumi
Insurance sales
City of Industry, CA

"If you look at your ceiling and see that it's peeling,
It's probably proof there's a leak in your roof."

John Kertland
Roofer
City of Industry, CA

"If muscle spasm and pain have you in grief,
Call Susan Hagman for hands-on relief."

Susan Hagman
Massage therapist
Diamond Bar, CA

"When the cops are in the foyer,
Call Marchese, your friendly lawyer."

David J. Marchese
Lawyer
Portland, ME

"The alchemist of old
Labored to turn lead to gold.
I turn plastic into cash!"

Hugh Byrne
Banker
Las Vegas, NV

"Please don't fret.
Please don't frown.

This Mary Kay Consultant
won't make you look like a clown!"

Betty Ann Wright
Cosmetics and skin care
Montebello, CA

"We lay for pay!"

Jim Hicks
Floor coverings
Sun Cities, AZ

"If they have a spine, they're mine."

Dr. Edward DiMaulo
Chiropractor
Scottsdale, AZ

"Reducing friction to a fraction
When you take action."

Joe Blanton
MaxiLube 2000
Las Vegas, NV

"Copies quick—You'll agree,
The folks to see are at Print Three!"

Richard Lyddon
Printer
Long Beach, CA

"You have to walk before you can run.
Call Pat Walker, she'll get it done!"

Pat Walker
Accounting and management services
Long Beach, CA

"Take pride in your ride."

Tony Dalia
Auto broker
Covina, CA

"We will fill, drill, and bill as painlessly as
possible."

Dr. Michael Tanaka
Dentist
Covina, CA

"Candy gives you cavities, flowers wilt and die,
So give a gift of jewelry to every mom and bride!"

Jeani Adams
Parklane Jewels
Anaheim, CA

"No one has endurance
Like the man who sells insurance."

Jeff Blake
Financial services
Boston, MA

"When you're overloaded
and just about to shout,

Don't completely lose your cool,
let Interim help you out!"

Rich Davenport
Interim Temporary Personnel
Montgomery, AL

"We'll yank your tank."

Rick Behrendt
Environmental engineering and consulting
Lansing, MI

"Don't let your back cramp your style—
Let us help restore that smile."

Dr. Don Wilkinson
Chiropractor
Montgomery, AL

"When your life is so hectic that your clothes
get neglected,

Don't dismay, call Advantage Valet."

Kathy Mallon
Valet services
Glendora, CA

"We find 'em, we bind 'em and we mind 'em
So our owners can leave their troubles behind 'em."

Alta Baker
Management group
Las Vegas, NV

"For colds or sniffles, call your M.D.;
For growth and life skills, please call me."

Maureen Kaczmarski, M.A.
Marriage and family counselor
Santa Ana, CA

"As my dear aunt once said,
'A little powder, a little paint
Can make a girl seem like she ain't.'"

Nena Anderson
Mary Kay Cosmetics
Las Vegas, NV

"We take care of your property properly
And don't take your casualty casually."

Jim Klocek
Farmers Insurance
Yucaipa, CA

"I can do loans that no one else can—
That's why they call me the Magic Man!"

George Beavin
Hawaii Federal Mortgage
Honolulu, HI

"BNI members get leads and grow;
Lock out your competition, so they won't know."

Steve York
Executive Director, BNI
Memphis, TN

121

*"From head to toe, inside out,
That's what your chiropractor cares about!"*

Dr. Chris Gaukler
Chiropractor
Orange, CA

*"As problems grow, the more you go
down life's long troubled journey,*

*Don't bitch and moan, get on the phone,
call Rich, the Business Network attorney."*

Richard Adams
Lawyer
Burbank, CA

C h a p t e r
11

Play with the Words

Get Them to Laugh As They Hand Over Their Business

MAYBE IT'S BECAUSE EVERYONE'S A COMEDIAN, but there seem to be more hooks involving word play than any other kind. There's a reason for it: tickling the funny bone is one of the friendliest ways to get the prospect's attention and good will. A customer who's laughing is a customer who's inclined to buy.

"You should be alarmed!"

Orville Barber
All Protection Security
Security systems
Inland Empire, CA

I am a young entrepreneur from South Central Los Angeles. I got the inspiration for this memory hook off a popular pizza ad, reworded it, and Eureka! A successful memory hook! I say successful because, since using it on door hangers, fliers, etc., throughout the Los Angeles area, I have generated 50 percent more business for the company.

A memory hook is worth a thousand words and thousands of dollars!

"We save dollars and make sense for your business."

Marc E. Rold
Business consultant
Torgerson Associates
Kalispell, MT

I have used this for nearly two years now. People remember me because I am the "dollars-and-sense guy." Since I work with an accounting firm, most people think of dollars and cents when they think of accounting, and a play on the old phrase is easy for people to remember. Who doesn't want to save dollars? The other part, about making sense, also appeals to many small-business people (my target market).

Most think that financial statements are just magic, but they want to understand them better and feel more in control of their business. If I can save them dollars and make sense out of something they find very confusing, I become their hero. This also give them a great way to introduce me to referrals they choose to make: "This is the guy who saves dollars and makes sense for me."

"Paying too much for overnight shipping services is not only a crime, it's a Federal offense!"

Owen S. Curry
UniShippers Association
Knoxville, TN

I am a broker of shipping services. The company whose services I broker the most is a competitor of Federal Express and UPS for overnight delivery of letters and small packages. Since FedEx owns about half of this market, their customers are my main target. I can provide services similar to theirs for about 40 percent less than their standard rates.

"If you have a single pane, we can double it and make you feel better!"

Vince Koach
Koach's Windows & Doors
Azusa, CA

After reading Dr. Misner's book *The World's Best Known Marketing Secret*, I realized I needed a memory hook. Not being able to come up with one myself, I enlisted the help of my family—we just happened to have a family gathering at that time. After I got several members of my family involved in the discussion, one of my sisters came up with the hook.

125

"Every good deed deserves a mortgage."

Don Humphrey
Waterfield Mortgage
Tarrytown, NY

Our commitment is to provide the borrower with the best service while continuing to offer some of the most competitive interest rates in the mortgage banking business. I wanted to try to impart this commitment to service and quality in my memory hook, and I came up with the thought that "every good deed deserves a mortgage." In the real estate business, "deeds" are crucial to each transaction. Without a deed, title cannot pass to a purchaser. But another, and equally important, good deed is the service that I can provide, backed by my company's resources. My "good deed"—professional commitment, service, and quality—will get each buyer a "good deed"—title to a new home with a Waterfield mortgage.

"A call to Stevens Van Lines will be the best move you'll ever make!"

Alan D. Cousino
Stevens Van Lines
Sylvania, OH

A few years ago our corporate office promoted the slogan "It's an easy move to make," in our sales literature. Most people believe that all moving companies are the same. I don't share that belief, and I wanted to convey some of that feeling in my hook, as well as the association of Stevens and "making the move." I am pleasantly surprised that this memory hook really does work. People I encounter remember most of it, but more importantly, they know what I do!

"If you feel like shooting your relatives, call Photos by Tom."

Tom Nanes
Photos by Tom
Las Vegas, NV

I am a professional photographer. I used this memory hook for about a year, then changed to a new one.

Recently I was being introduced to someone I didn't recognize. He suddenly shouted out, "Oh! You're the one that shoots relatives. I heard your hook last year and it stuck in my mind." I still couldn't remember meeting the person.

Two days later another person I didn't recognize yelled out across a room, "Still shooting relatives?" It was in front of five other people, and everyone started laughing.

Twice in one week, my old memory hook had been used by two people I really didn't know—so I immediately changed back to that memory hook. Everyone chuckles now when I use it. Each week I show one enlargement of my current photo work.

"We do good deeds."

Shane Liedtke
Meridian Title Company
Murray, UT

I can't take credit for the creation of this memory hook. It was created by a secretary who worked for us long ago. At that time we began using it on all our mailings, business cards, stationery, and other correspondence materials.

I started using it in our weekly meetings. One week we introduced not ourselves but another member in the group, and Dixie Marelli introduced me as the "Boy Scout of Title" because I do "good deeds." I've now used that as my memory hook as well; I tell the people I meet that I am the Boy Scout of Title because I do good deeds, and that I am honest, thrifty, brave (enough to get the job done right), courteous, and kind in all my closings and in my association with my clients (and others).

"Caring, Practical, and Affordable"

"Need the facts about tax? Call Mrs. J today!"

Catherine M. Janowicz
Certified Public Accountant
La Habra, CA

When I give my fifteen-minute talk, I try to give a CPA-related door prize—usually, a calculator. After years of searching, I found a high-quality pocket calculator that could be imprinted. Besides the usual name, address, telephone number, and accounting and tax services imprint, I wanted a memory hook that sounded professional, yet conveyed my "warm, cozy, and down-to-earth" self.

So "Caring, Practical, and Affordable" came into being. Catchy because of the CPA initials, yes, but it is also me.

I use this memory hook when I introduce myself during my 60-second commercial at networking meetings. It is the basis for a great chat about my practice and where I am coming from. "Caring, Practical, and Affordable" has been well received, especially as a visual aid.

Since I do not consider myself the typical boring, bean-counter CPA, I wanted a warm, cozy, down-to-earth memory hook. My children's friends have lovingly called me "Mrs. J" for years. I also enjoy doing taxes and explaining to clients all the income tax facts necessary for their particular situation. So—"facts about tax."

I am also an accountant, and I provide all types of bookkeeping and accounting services. So, occasionally, I will add the following memory hook: "Books need a look or need the facts about tax? Call Mrs. J today!" This hook has worked equally well, and I use one or the other depending on what I am talking about that day.

"Try us before they try you."

Martin A. Clayman
Lawyer
Clayman, Markowitz, Pinney & Baram, L.L.C.
Bloomfield, CT

This memory hook occurred to me because I have always stressed and encouraged the prevention of legal problems. All too frequently, clients face lawsuits because of their neglect or ignorance of the law. I know that it is far less expensive to anticipate legal pitfalls than to fall into them.

I want to give my clients, and potential clients, a short, clear message that they can understand. Most people know that litigation is costly, and it is usually cost-effective to consult with a capable attorney who can guide the client through the maze of complex laws and regulations.

I am planning to use this memory hook in connection with a legal audit program that I intend to launch in the near future with my business clients.

"Let's make a wheel!"

Philip M. Fitzpatrick
Auto leasing agent
Brent Leasing
Markham, Ontario, Canada

Originally we wanted a short, concise memory hook that made a statement—something that would be a play on words, as some of the most effective memory hooks have been. We wanted people to know we were prepared to create a fair deal, anywhere, anytime, and on any vehicle.

A further parallel we thought of was "What goes around comes around." This is the basis of referral, and, like a wheel, it goes around—a memory hook with backup support! Our business has benefited, and our referrals have benefited other members from the network.

"Computer Junction, where megabytes don't cost megabucks."

Gary P. Jochum
Computer Junction
Carbondale, CO

In the highly competitive marketplace of high-tech computer sales, there is a misconception that a shopper must go to the big discount houses to get the best price deals. Aside from the fact that the "Wal-Marts" don't offer any real technical support after the sale is completed, we wanted our customers to know not only that we do give them customer support, but that they don't have to pay more to get it.

We live in a small mountain valley; consumers typically go to Grand Junction or Denver or order by mail to obtain their hardware. We wanted them at least to consider Computer Junction and weigh the differences.

**"Mine is an easy memory hook—
CALL REED to print any kind of specialty BOOK."**

Reed Morgan
Jostens Printing & Publishing Division
Nashville, TN

As a BNI director, I have tried to use a memory hook that incorporated a descriptor of my business, a clever rhyme, and a good example of a hook that works. My members do use it to find leads for me. This hook is now included on my business cards, which certainly helps tell what kind of work this printer does.

"I'm the LOAN ArRANGER."

Bob Sutterfield
Hawaii Federal Mortgage
Honolulu, HI

Bob often plays the *William Tell Overture* on a cassette deck while giving his memory hook and talking about his business. He's been using this hook for over nine years. People love it! He says they always remember him and sometimes address him as the "Loan Arranger" instead of "Bob."

"Would you rather sink your teeth into a tasty meal, or a glass of water on the nightstand?"

Dr. Larry R. Paul
Dentist
San Diego, CA

I was reading through some dental material and the idea hit me. It was an epiphany! I used it on our network group and got oohs and aahs . . . and they remembered it!

There are many more examples of word play in memory hooks, all creative and all compelling.

"Opportunity doesn't knock, it rings."

Paul Broyles
Excel Telecommunications
Long-distance phone service
Chattanooga, TN

"Loans with your best interest in mind."

Jeffrey C. Negus
Mortgage broker
Jefferson Mortgage Capital
Mission Viejo, CA

"We add a touch of glass."

Kevin Hansen
Custom Glass
Moreno Valley, CA

"We check your shorts."

Dean Georgianna
Electrician
Yucaipa, CA

"Tulips are better than one!"

Irene Bailey
Florist
Huntington Beach, CA

"Be patient with me, you're dealing with a basket case!"

Lynne Whelan
Gift baskets
Las Vegas, NV

"If your hair is not becoming to you, then you should be coming to me."

Joey Reid
Hair salon
Covina, CA

"I can handle your type anytime."

Avis Jacobson
Word processing service
Huntington Beach, CA

"Come chew the fat with me."

Mike Keith
Diet center
Moreno Valley, CA

"Come fly away with me."

Micky Sadil
Travel agent
Moreno Valley, CA

"Bring your swing and let us fix it."

Ron Kennedy
Golf professional
Costa Mesa, CA

"We'll take care of anything that's bugging you!"

Larry Habben
Exterminator
Tustin, CA

"We'd like a crack at your business!"

Joel Morse
Windshield repair
Anaheim, CA

"Think of me as your local call girl!"

Karen McElwain
Cellular phones
Newport Beach, CA

"We won't steam you up!"

Ted Cortez
Carpet cleaner
Yucaipa, CA

"To shine or not to shine, that is the question."

Jim Davis
Auto detailer
Laguna Hills, CA

"Don't get caught with your data down!"

Paula Meierle
Complete Computer Communication
Huntington Beach, CA

"If you need to be kneaded, then you need me."

Pamela Doxat-Parker
Massage therapist
Beverly Hills, CA

"Think of us when you meet someone by accident!"

Olga Shrewsbury
Auto collision repair
Huntington Beach, CA

"There is life after debt!"

Walter López
Credit negotiations
Corona, CA

"Let us floor you."

Linda Bratrud
Floor coverings
East Valley, AZ

"Come and see me; I want to get on your nerves."

Dr. Marcy Dionisio
Chiropractor
East Valley, AZ

"Our office will keep you a foot above the rest."

Dr. Steven Rovall
Podiatric physician
Salt Lake City, UT

"If you know someone who would like to save on taxes, tell them to see Robert Wagoner, or face the Taxequences!"

Robert Wagoner
Financial planner
Santa Ana, CA

"I am the underground real estate agent. We want to be the last ones to let you down."

Jay Poster
Prearrangement funeral counselor
Las Vegas, NV

"See Osterberg & Associates for many happy returns!"

Gary Osterberg
Certified Public Accountant
Long Beach, CA

"No business ever died from overexposure—so expose yourself!"

Jeff Deming
Advertising
Cottonwood, AZ

"At Betts Carpet Care, we're dyeing to save you money."

Zachary Betts
Carpet care and dyeing
Santa Ana, CA

"May the floss be with you!"

Dr. Michael Giovannini
Dentist
Lancaster, CA

"I spy for you."

Allen Imig
Private investigator
Foothills, AZ

"If you want to get rubbed the right way, see Jim."

Jim Wagner
Massage technician
Redmond, WA

"If your back is going out more often than you are, you need to see me."

Dr. Robert Caires
Chiropractor
Honolulu, HI

"I do what people don't like to do. I do Windows!"

Douglas Roshong
Computer service
Sylvania, OH

"We go the extra mile to give you a yard."

Robert Simmons
Landscaping
Moreno Valley, CA

"I don't want your whole body—just your tows."

Brent Rikes
Automotive repair and towing
South Orlando, FL

"Old bankers never die—they just lose interest."

Thomas Quirk
Banker
White Plains, NY

"We want to get you in hot water!"

Bill Scott
Hot tubs
Sevier County, TN

"We make your floors reflect well on you."

Jerry Wallace
Commercial floor care
Oak Ridge, TN

"Painting the town, one house at a time."

Kelli Holmes
Holmes Painting
La Verne, CA

"For the 'Honey, dos' your honey doesn't."

Paul Richardson
Handy Man Service
Denver, CO

"Missing breakfast can be hazardous to your wealth."

Bruce Elliott
Executive Director, BNI
S. W. Ontario, Canada

"I put the 'person' in your personnel!"

Howard S. Wenger
Account executive
Business Systems Staffing & Associates, Inc.
Los Angeles, CA

"Washington is Evergreen because it's raining leads!"

Lee M. Blackwell
Executive Director, BNI
Seattle/Tacoma, WA

"Hi, my name is Kathy Mathy. I'm a CPA, and I run an Intensive Care 'DE-TAX' Unit."

Kathleen A. Mathy
Certified Public Accountant
Sugar Land, TX

"If you want a better piece of chicken . . . you'd have to be a rooster!"

Rick Kambestad
Multi-Foods Inc.
Atascadero, CA

"Glad to see your back."

Dr. Ted Peña
Chiropractor
Canyon Springs, CA

"Buy a filter or be a filter."

Dan Rawls
NSA Water & Air Filters
Knoxville, TN

"I fix floppy discs!"

Dr. Dean Dryer
Chiropractor
Laguna Hills, CA

"Trading a penny for a dollar always makes more sense."

Nicholas Yuschenkoff
Principal Financial Group
Costa Mesa, CA

"For the little things that bug you, give me a call."

Leroy Quintana
Pest control
Huntington Beach, CA

"I have your best interest in mind."

William Souve
Mortgage banker
Newport Beach, CA

"Be true to your teeth or they will be false to you."

Dr. Paul S. Kozy
Dentist
Toledo, OH

Chapter
12

Take the
Next Step

*Using What
You've Learned*

WHAT YOU'VE JUST SEEN is only a sampling of the many excellent memory hooks friends and colleagues in a grand range of businesses have sent me. If you sent one that was left out, never fear; there will be more editions of this book with more memory hooks to entertain and enlighten you, and yours may well be among the next batch.

One of the things you've probably noticed is how coming up with a memory hook unleashes the imagination and brings out the creativity in people. Most of those interviewed indicated that it was a lot of fun to invent and present their memory hooks. This kind of creative stimulation is good for your business in other ways as well. When you start thinking of new ways to grab a prospect's attention, you often gain new insights into how to improve your business, expand your range of products or services, lower your costs, and increase your profit margins. Once you open yourself up to new ways of thinking, your friends, family, employees, sometimes even your competitors can help you see your business with new eyes.

> *When you start thinking about new ways to grab a prospect's attention, you often gain insight into other ways to improve your business.*

BAIT YOUR OWN HOOK

NOW IT'S TIME FOR YOU TO COME UP with your own memory hook, using the principles and examples I've given you. Part III contains a number of tools that can help you create your hook. You may find the form on page 153 useful in fitting your memory hook into your 60-second presentation. As for creating the hook, ask yourself what unique or outstanding aspects of your business you wish to bring to the prospect's attention. The index of memory hooks by profession (p. 155) shows you how others in your line of work have answered this question for themselves and may give you ideas about your own approach.

Why use a memory hook? It's a way of drawing attention quickly to your commercial message, especially in a person-to-person or a person-to-group situation. When you use a memory hook, you set yourself up to be remembered; and when you are remembered, people will refer you to other people who are then more likely to buy your products or use your professional services.

How does a memory hook work? As storytellers, wandering minstrels, singers, and writers have known for centuries, certain characteristics of language have a universal appeal. If you frame your statement about yourself in particular ways, you are almost guaranteed the listener's attention. When you invent your memory hook, keep in mind one or more of these basic guidelines:

1. Make it short and vivid.

2. Appeal to the senses: sight, hearing, taste, smell, touch.

3. Make it funny—or make it touching.

4. Make it rhyme (or make it a song).

5. Parody something familiar.

6. Make a two-part statement.

Use your creative energy as well to increase your networking. Remember, the best use of a memory hook is to leverage your most productive marketing tool—word of mouth. Referrals build on each other to get word to people who want to know what products and services their friends and colleagues like the best; the memory hook ties those products and services irrevocably to you. Maximize your contacts; attend regular meetings of networking and professional groups; find new ways of networking. It will pay off handsomely.

> *The best use of a memory hook is to leverage your most productive marketing tool—word of mouth.*

Polish your self-presentation, both for individual meetings and for groups. Think of ways to grab your audience's attention. Strive to engage positively the interest of your prospects. Remember the photographer who accents his hook, "We preserve memories in a flash!" by firing a strobe at his audience? That is one way to make an indelible

impression. With a little time for skylarking or a brainstorm-
ing session with your friends, perhaps you can come up with
one suitable for your business.

Use your hook on as many kinds of marketing materials
as you can. That way, if someone comes across your business
card or calendar or one of your ballpoint pens, that person
will automatically associate it with something someone said
about you, even if you haven't met. Try to establish an
unbreakable connection between your memory hook and
your business.

SHOW US YOURS

SOON YOU WILL HAVE CREATED your own memory hook. Try
it out on individuals, in meetings, on your marketing materials. Then, using the form on page 154, write and tell me how
it works. This will help me compile a future edition of this
book, which will in turn help yet more enterprising business-
men and businesswomen get the word out about their products and services. And, not incidentally, it may get you
mentioned in a book that you can use to show your children
and grandchildren what you did in the great marketing
wars.

Oh, by the way, for those of you wondering what my
memory hook is . . . just remember that when you're trying
to build your business through word of mouth, it's not
NET-SIT or NET-EAT, it's NETWORK!

Part
III

Hands On

*Tools to Help You Create and
Share Your Own Memory Hook*

PART III

NOTES

▼

WORKSHEETS

▼

INDEX OF MEMORY HOOKS BY PROFESSION

▼

ABOUT BUSINESS NETWORK INT'L.

▼

NOTES

CHAPTER 2

1. John Naisbitt, *Megatrends: Ten New Directions Transforming Our Lives* (New York: Warner Books, 1982).

2. American Entrepreneur Association, *Making Ads Pay: Advertising Techniques for Small Businesses,* AEA Business Special Report (Los Angeles: AEA, 1985), pp. 3324–25.

3. Richard Engdahl, Vince Howe, and Donald Cole, "Marketing O.D.: What Now Works and What Does Not," *Organizational Development Journal* (Organizational Development Institute, Summer 1991, p. 36).

4. McGraw-Hill tells us that the average salesman's call costs $178, a letter $6.63 and a phone call $6.35 (David Ogilvy, *Ogilvy on Advertising*, New York: Crown Publishers, 1983, p. 137).

5. Engdahl, Howe, and Cole, p. 37.

6. Tom Peters, *Thriving on Chaos* (New York: Alfred A. Knopf, 1987), p. 242.

7. When I suggested teaching a course in face-to-face sales and networking, the science and art of marketing directly to the consumer, the department head at the university where I taught said, "We don't teach that kind of thing here." Apparently it's too real-world, too hands-on. They'd rather continue teaching what I call "sterile sales," case studies on top-echelon decision making at Procter & Gamble and IBM, as though small-business sales and big-business salespeople didn't exist.

8. Jim and JoAnn Carland, *Small Business Management* (PWS-Kent Publishing, Boston, 1990), p. 5.

9. Why are sales seminar gurus like Tom Hopkins and Brian Tracy doing so well today? Besides the fact that they are great educators and have a good message, our colleges are churning out graduates who don't have a clue about how to market directly to the consumer. This creates an instant after-college market for business and sales training that encompasses even specialized professions such as health, law, and accounting. I've talked to hundreds of health care professionals, lawyers, and accountants who told me they were taught only how to provide their services—not a word about how to sell their services to the consumer.

10. Maybe someday, when we can sit at home and hold a meeting with holographic images of ten other business people around our kitchen table, we won't feel we need to leave the office to have human contact—but I doubt it. Besides, you can't get a haircut by phone.

11. Engdahl, Howe, and Cole, p. 36.

12. At the time of this printing, BNI alone has over six hundred chapters.

13. "L.A. Connects Westside/Downtown," *The Directory of Networking Organizations, 1996 Edition* (Los Angeles: L.A. Connects, 1996). According to the same article, a referral generates 80 percent more results than a cold call.

CHAPTER 3

1. Thirty seconds is not a hard-and-fast rule, of course. According to L.A. Connects, for instance, "A sale is won or lost during the first 90 seconds of a salesperson's introduction" (*Directory of Networking Organizations*, p. 17).

2. Norman King, *The First Five Minutes: The Successful Opening Moves in Business, Sales & Interviews* (New York: Prentice-Hall Press, 1987), pp. 1, 8.

3. Milo O. Frank, *How to Get Your Point Across in 30 Seconds or Less* (New York: Pocket Books, 1986), p. 15.

4. Donna Fisher and Sandy Vilas, *Power Networking: 55 Secrets for Personal & Professional Success* (Austin: MountainHarbour Publications, 1992), p. 75.

5. It is often more comfortable to be introduced by a third person, especially someone who knows both of you. The introducer can tell your new acquaintance what you do and, not being constrained by modesty, can say better things about you than you could safely say about yourself.

6. Fisher and Vilas, pp. 77–78.

7. Leonard Zunin, *Contact* (New York: Ballantine, 1992).

8. Susan RoAne, *How to Work a Room* (New York: Warner Books, 1991).

9. Fisher and Vilas, pp. 79–80.

10. Bob Burg, *Endless Referrals: Network Your Everyday Contacts* (New York: McGraw-Hill, 1994), p. 84.

11. Erna Cutlip, Nancy Center, and Betty Broom, *Effective Public Relations* (Englewood Cliffs, New Jersey: Prentice-Hall, 1985), p. 178.

12. King, p. 1.

13. Kerry Johnson, "The Battle for Your Prospect's Mind," *Broker World* (July 1989, p. 86).

14. Joyce Hadley and Betsy Sheldon, *The Smart Woman's Guide to Networking* (Franklin Lakes, New Jersey: Career Press, 1995), p. 182.

15. American Entrepreneur Association, pp. 3324–25.

CHAPTER 4

1. Anne Baber and Lynn Waymon, *Great Connections: Small Talk and Networking for Businesspeople* (Manassas Park, Virginia: Impact Publications, 1992), p. 89.

2. Ron Sukenick, *Networking Your Way to Success* (Dubuque, Iowa: Kendall/Hunt, 1995), p. 70.

CHAPTER 6

1. Answers: Sprint, Ajax, and Maxwell House.

ANATOMY OF A 60-SECOND PRESENTATION

A good 60-second presentation consists of five parts. Use this worksheet to develop the best 60-second presentation imaginable. Fill out one of these for each week. Read it verbatim, memorize it, or improvise from it.

1. The introduction:
My name is _____, and I'm with _____ .

2. The memory hook. Good memory hooks are memorable, descriptive, and short. Be creative.

_____

_____

3. The body. This portion constitutes the majority of the presentation and will be thirty to forty-five seconds. Ideally, you should deliver a different body each week. Focus on one service or product; discuss the benefits of the service rather than the service itself. Also discuss what constitutes a good lead for you.

_____

_____

_____

_____

_____

_____

4. The summation. In one or two short sentences, reiterate what you've just said, stating the reasons to act now!

_____

_____

_____

5. The closing. State one more time your name and the name of your company:
I'm _____ with _____ .

SEND US YOUR MEMORY HOOK

Dr. Ivan Misner will be publishing new editions of this book in the not-too-distant future. If you would like to have your memory hook considered for the next edition, please complete this form and mail it—or, better yet, fax it—to Dr. Misner. You may include more than one memory hook. If you need more room, please attach another sheet.

1. Write your memory hook(s).

2. What led you to create this memory hook?

3. How do people react to your memory hook?

4. If you have a funny, interesting, or success-related story regarding the use of memory hooks, please describe.

Your name: _____

Company name: _____

Your profession: _____

Business address: _____

Business phone: _____

Call 1-800-688-9394 for our fax number, or mail to BNI, 199 South Monte Vista, San Dimas, CA 91773 (e-mail: misner@bninet.com).

▼

INDEX OF MEMORY HOOKS
BY PROFESSION

This index categorizes memory hooks by profession or business and, to help you locate a memory hook that you are trying to remember, by the name of the person who submitted it, regardless of whether that person is the owner or operator of the business.

Accounting and tax services
Kris Krauskopf 63
Joyce Guerrera 68
Robert L. Kailes 70
Mark Guillod 75
Russ Whitehouse 79
Lucygne O'ffill 81
Scott Pierson 82
C. Trevor McMurray 95
Linda Brown 100
Stephanie Roderick 113
Wendy Martin 115
Pat Walker 118
Catherine M. Janowicz 128
Gary Osterberg 137
Kathleen A. Mathy 141

Advertising
Jim Walters 57
Jane M. White 59
Ray DeLeone 73
Dave Voracek 86
Dennis R. Green 110
Jeff Deming 137

Air conditioning and heating
Tim Sweat 52
Jim Lakner 74

Automobile sales and leasing
Tony Dalia 118
Philip M. Fitzpatrick 130

Automobile service
Ian Melmed 77
Lisa Boushey 108

Joe Blanton 117
Joel Morse 134
Jim Davis 135
Olga Shrewsbury 136
Brent Rikes 139

Balloons
Steve Kromer 113

Banking
Hugh Byrne 116
Thomas Quirk 139

Bartenders
R. David Hackenbruch 78

Building contractors
Ralph Jones 56
Bob Baker 91
David Koller 91
Ken McCarthy 113
John Kertland 116
Jim Hicks 117
Vince Koach 125
Dean Georgianna 133
Linda Bratrud 136
Kelli Holmes 140

Business networking
Candace Bailly 83
J. R. Chick Gallagher 83
Don Morgan 83
K. Lynn Morgan 83
Norm Dominguez 87
John R. Meyer 89
Susan Butler 92
Elisabeth Misner 92

Business networking (continued)
Alice Ostrower 96
Andra Brack 97
Penny Palmer 104
Steve York 121
Bruce Elliott 140
Lee M. Blackwell 141

Catering and food services
Carol Zapadka 77
Rick Kambestad 141

Chiropractors
Ken Cragen 62
Catherine Devore 75
John A. Vogel 99
Diane Bellwood 112
Edward DiMaulo 117
Don Wilkinson 120
Chris Gaukler 122
Marcy Dionisio 136
Robert Caires 138
Ted Peña 141
Dean Dryer 142

Cleaning services
Becky Mays 55
Scott Pedrick 60
Diane Licciardi 74
Barbara Kinkade 76
Jeanne Ainsley 91
Debbie Haun 91
Ardiss McDonald,
    Marlin Fisher 100
Flory Kemp Peterson,
    Sharyl McGowan 110
Ted Cortez 135
Zachary Betts 138
Jerry Wallace 140

Communication services.
See Telephones

Computers
Vandar and Zena Awesome .. 48
Robert McNutt 76
Sally Dicken 79
Patrick LaBash 80
Gary P. Jochum 130
Paula Meierle 135
Douglas Roshong 139

Cosmetics
Jan Scott 60
Mary Whitman 73
Rennie Kesterson 77
Stephanie Lara 98
Betty Ann Wright 117
Nena Anderson 121

Credit and debt services
Susan Parker 114
Walter López 136

Dentists
Joe Wilson 73
Victoria Outmans 75
Pat Lester 76
Alan Miller 99
Renee Mullins 107
Larry Brown 112
Rosellen Kimbrough 114
Michael Tanaka 118
Larry R. Paul 132
Michael Giovannini 138
Paul S. Kozy 142

Desktop publishing. See Graphic
design and desktop publishing

Dietitians
Mike Keith 134

Engineering
Coleman Moore 96
Rick Behrendt 119

Exterminators
Larry Habben 134
Leroy Quintana 142

Filters, water and air
Dan Rawls 141

Financial planning and
investments
Bob Carroll 60
Philip Heyl 60
Joyce Theis 67
Tom Hanson 75
Edward D. Jones 78
Bob Cullen 80
John Miller 84
Diane Haneklau 95
Catherine Herod 100

Marjorie Stanford 112
Robert Wagoner 137

Financial services, general
John Nichols 52
Martha E. Laff 70
James R. Larew 100
Nicholas Yuschenkoff 142

Florists
Brenda Berkery 64
Andrea Kramer 84
Irene Bailey 133

Gifts
Diane Verdaasdonk 77
Lynne Whelan 133

Glass
Kevin Hansen 132

Golf professionals
Ron Kennedy 134

Graphic design and desktop
publishing
Dorothy Winkel 74
Richard Scoby 82
Jacque Foreman 102
Avis Jacobson 133

Hair stylists
Christine Stock 82
Janet Rios 111
Joey Reid 133

Handyman services
Paul Richardson 140

Hot tubs
Bill Scott 139

Household goods
Vicki Bart 111

Insurance
Larry Nold 49
David Machry 67
Jack Knight 73
Anne Wertz 74
Frank Jones 77
Al Sutton 80
Joy Jones 88
Lee Ann Zerbel 99
Joe Hansen 104

Marsha Aizumi 115
Jeff Blake 119
Jim Klocek 121

Jewelry
Jeani Adams 119

Landscaping and lawn care
John Laney 92
Robert Simmons 139

Legal services
Marc Simon 52
Thomas W. Teixeira 71
Raymond Arenofsky 80
Brian Daily 81
Sue Kraft 113
Gloria Jones 115
David J. Marchese 116
Richard Adams 122
Martin A. Clayman 129

Management services
Alta Baker 120
Marc E. Rold 124

Massage therapists
Sharon Howard 72
Susan Hagman 116
Pamela Doxat-Parker 135
Jim Wagner 138

Mortgage lending
Bob Howe 52
Pat McCormick 66
Jim Nassar 106
Steve Marche 109
George Beavin 121
Don Humphrey 126
Bob Sutterfield 131
Jeffrey C. Negus 132
William Souve 142

Mortuary services
Stanley Pulver Jr. 79
Jay Poster 137

Movers
Wayne LaMade 78
Russ Roman 90
Alan D. Cousino 126

Musicians
Doug Taylor 82

Office furniture
Scott Epstein 54

Office supplies
Mollie Green 66

Optometrists
Mel Honda 52

Personnel services
Rich Davenport 119
Howard S. Wenger 140

Pest control. *See* Exterminators

Photography
Marvin L. Jeffreys 58
Robert Stewart 71
Tom Nanes 127

Physical training
Jeffry C. Hoy 94
Gary Brownlee 99

Podiatrists
Steven Rovall 136

Printing and graphics services
Kevin L. Pasternack 60
Diane Barretti 65
Oscar Bovolini 81
Donald E. Hart 89
Bruce Davis 91
Richard Lyddon 118
Reed Morgan 131

Private investigators
Allen Imig 138

Psychological services
Linda Garcia 74
Edward J. Waters 79
Marty Renger 98
Maureen Kaczmarski 120

Radio broadcasting
Lisa Meades 56

Real estate
Unknown 41
Roberta Wright 50
Les Harris 51
Kathy Paugh 75
Barbara Karvelas 78
Barbara Grimes 81

Security services
Paul Ryan 112
Orville Barber 124

Shipping services
Owen S. Curry 125

Tax services. *See* Accounting
and tax services

Telephones
Dick Rieke 59
Deena Regier 76
Jackie Maugh 80
Paul Broyles 132
Karen McElwain 135

Title services
Shane Liedtke 127

Travel agents
Leni Maier 68
Lance Mead 69
Pat Yee 73
Rosemary Hall 76
Sharrie Long 105
Micky Sadil 134

Typesetting. *See* Graphic design
and desktop publishing

Valet services
Kathy Mallon 120

Video services
Howard Greenspon 90
Craig and Linda Campana .. 92

Window tinting
Mary Rousseve 108

Word processing. *See* Graphic
design and desktop publishing

▼
ABOUT BUSINESS NETWORK INT'L.

BUSINESS NETWORK INT'L. (BNI) was founded by Dr. Ivan Misner in 1985 as a way for business people to generate referrals in a structured, professional environment. BNI is now the largest referral networking organization of its kind in the world, with thousands of members in more than six hundred chapters. Since its inception, BNI members have passed over 1.5 million referrals, generating over half a billion dollars in business for the participants.

The primary purpose of the organization is to pass qualified business referrals to the members. The philosophy of BNI may be summed up in two simple words: Givers Gain. If you give business to people, you will get business from them. BNI allows only one person per profession to join a chapter. The program is designed for business people to develop long-term relationships, thereby creating a basis for trust and, inevitably, referrals. The mission of the organization is to teach business professionals that the word-of-mouth process is more about farming than it is hunting: it's about the cultivation of professional relationships in a structured business environment for the mutual benefit of all.

To get more information on a chapter in your area, call 1-800-688-9394 or visit BNI's home page at www.bninet.com.

FOR ADDITIONAL COPIES OF

7 SECOND MARKETING

How to Use Memory Hooks to Make You Instantly Stand Out in a Crowd

Hardcover	**$22.95**
Paperback	**$12.95**

OR FOR COPIES OF

THE WORLD'S BEST KNOWN MARKETING SECRET

Building Your Business with Word-of-Mouth Marketing

Hardcover	**$24.95**
Paperback	**$14.95**

CALL TOLL FREE

1-800-688-9394

24 HOURS A DAY

7 DAYS A WEEK

QUANTITY DISCOUNTS ARE AVAILABLE.

VISA/MASTERCARD/AMERICAN EXPRESS

TO ORDER BY MAIL,

ENCLOSE CHECK WITH YOUR ORDER PAYABLE TO

PARADIGM PRODUCTIONS
199 SOUTH MONTE VISTA
SAN DIMAS, CA 91773